What People Are Saying About
Cleaning and the Meaning of Life . . .

"I highly recommend this bright and powerful book for clearing clutter and bringing joy to our lives."

—**Alexandra Stoddard**
Things I Want My Daughters to Know

"*Cleaning and the Meaning of Life* is a fun, fabulous read filled with simple tips to make your life lighter and brighter. We love, love, loved this book."

—**Jennifer and Kitty O'Neil**
Decorating with Funky Shui

"Who knew a pragmatic organizing tome could be could be a page turner? Jhung's straightforward strategies will resonate for anyone who wants to bring order to a chaotic home."

—**Lisa Skolnik, Chicago City Editor**
Metropolitan Home magazine

"Written with Paula Jhung's trademark wit and humor, this delightful book brims with clever ideas and fun-to-use tips."

—**Harriet Schechter**
Let Go of Clutter

"What I love most about *Cleaning and the Meaning of Life* is the creative approach it takes tackling a basic topic—cleaning. Hundreds of times while reading it I would smack my forehead and say, 'Man, that's such a great idea. I wish I had written that.'"

—**Lee Silber**
Organizing from the Right Side of the Brain

"*Cleaning and the Meaning of Life* is an enlightening guidebook to joyful, healthy, clean living. Whether you dread cleaning house or adore tidying up, you'll gain a sense of freedom and empowerment from the simple, profound insights that fill these pages."

—**Taro Gold**

Living Wabi Sabi

Cleaning and the Meaning of Life

Simple Solutions to Declutter Your Home and Beautify Your Life

Paula Jhung

Health Communications, Inc.
Deerfield Beach, Florida

www.hcibooks.com

Library of Congress Cataloging-in-Publication Data

Jhung, Paula.
    Cleaning and the meaning of life : simple solutions to declutter your home
and beautify your life / Paula Jhung.
        p. cm.
    ISBN 0-7573-0240-8 (tp)
    1. House cleaning. I. Title.

    TX324.J45 2005
    648'.5—dc22
                                                                2005040313

Publisher: Health Communications, Inc.
          3201 S.W. 15th Street
          Deerfield Beach, FL 33442-8190

Cover design by Larissa Hise Henoch
Inside book design by Lawna Patterson Oldfield

To Larry, Kelley and Lisa
who continually show me
what's it all about.

Contents

Part IV: Enhance Flow: Cultivate Inner Comforts

Acknowledgments

Just as particular people give meaning to life, they've given life to this book. They include literary agent Janet Rosen who not only opened the door but also explored many nooks and crannies with me. I'm also grateful to HCI's Kim Weiss for the hoopla and hard work, and to my editor, Allison Janse, whose fine-tuning and gentle pruning helped me say what I had to say.

A special thanks to the friends and family who provided ideas, inspiration, contacts, feedback, support and/or down-home psychotherapy. They include Liz Seibold, Carol Coburn, Jane Carlin, Ilene Spector, Carol Doughty, Donna Dixon, Dorothy Mann, Barbara von Rosen, Jane Cramer, Kaye Dutrow, the late Alden Pearce, Lee Silber, Barbara Cansino Kaufman, Julia Richmond, Eileen Tichenor-Doak, Vivien Mayer, Lorraine Telnak, Chris Sykes, Barbara Riccio, Mary Chaisson, and Larry, Kelley and Lisa Jhung.

My everlasting gratitude to John Seibold and especially Lee Dewey for keeping me plugged in, and to Juana Rivera for keeping me cleaned up. And to the many experts who gave ideas the credibility, including psychologists John Gray, John Rosemond and Gita Morena; organizing experts Julie Morgenstern and Harriet Schechter; architect Carol Venolia; interior designers Alexandra Stoddard and Marie Kinnaman; clothing expert Steve Boorstien;

and furniture restorer and Oxford University decorative arts tutor Amy Buxton.

"Gratitude is the memory of the heart."

—J.B. Massieu

Introduction:
What's It All About?

The Problem

Life is messy. Dirt gets tracked on the floors, dust drifts in through the windows, dog hair covers the easy chair, drinks get sloshed on the sofa and debris piles up anywhere it wants to.

Yet if we're going to make the most of the time we have on this planet, we need a clean, comfortable, uplifting home from which to operate. After all, home is the base that bolsters all we do, whether we're rearing a boisterous family or living a life of quiet retreat.

Cleaning and the Meaning of Life details simple ways to pare down and lighten up. It also shows how to increase comfort, enhance flow and create surroundings that are not only a snap to maintain, they uplift the soul and reflect the very best of who we are.

I've long fought what I saw as the bondage of home care, but I've discovered over time that certain aspects of it can be almost spiritual, especially if we approach it as a way to add beauty, grace and renewal to our lives. There is release to be found in purging a closet, pleasure in sleeping on sun-dried sheets and delight in arranging a pitcher of lilacs.

There are odious jobs, of course, like getting gunk out of sliding door tracks and scouring the floor around the toilet, but my approach to cleaning is more preventive than prescriptive.

But let's make this perfectly clear: I'm no clean freak. Ever since I was a child, when I was regularly grounded for the abominable state of my room, I've been obsessed by housework. Not doing it. Dodging it.

I hated cleaning, but the more I'd let things slide, the crummier I'd feel. I also looked pretty rumpled myself, since I'd lose shoes, underwear and whole outfits among the rubble.

When forced by the in-house health department, known as Mom, to clean up my act, a funny thing happened—my outlook and my life improved. By controlling the disorder, I felt in control and confident. But since my lazy streak runs long and deep, the power never lasted. In time, I knew I would have to find a more creative plan to manage my stuff and master my life.

It didn't come easily. I became a flight attendant back in the days of airline spit and polish, when every hair had to be in place and every nail perfectly manicured. Even in the boot camp of the flight academy, drawers, closets and beds were checked daily for tidiness. Through some miracle, I was able to fake my way through it. When I finally got my probationary wings, I was the target of persnickety supervisors who hassled me for everything from my sloppy purse to the dog-eared condition of my flight service manual. I got my share of warning notices, but believe me, I survived because I kept a smile plastered on my face at all times, partly because I knew they couldn't check out the condition of my pigpen apartment.

I may have been a slob, but I craved supportive surroundings like I craved a supportive partner. Both had to be good looking, fun, forgiving and comfortable to be around. What I didn't want from either was high maintenance. I got lucky with the partner, but the surroundings proved to be more challenging.

Motherhood made home tending even harder. Keeping track of

my own stuff was bad enough, but little dependents as well? I'm still amazed I didn't misplace one of them along with their diapers, rattles, blankets and everything else I seemed to litter about.

But something shifted the day I went back to school to study interior design. I desperately needed a system to balance home life while keeping track of the reams of paper, fabrics and books I was bombarded with. I also figured this was where I could find a way to outwit the dirt and debris that both slowed me up and brought me down.

While more ambitious students strove to make their marks on the design world, I concentrated on preventing marks, or at least camouflaging them with color and pattern. I also learned how to separate the wheat from the chaff of possessions, while keeping the whole look warm, personal and comfortable.

In the process, I discovered that small improvements could be mood brightening and even life changing. Waking up in a cheerful bedroom, having easy access to a well-tended wardrobe and getting the family off without the usual morning chaos boost one's outlook and confidence all day. And coming home to warmly lit, well-ordered, super comfy surroundings soothes even the most stressed soul.

My new know-how not only helped clean up my act and improve it, it also led to a career in easy-care, life-transforming decorating as well as inspired hundreds of magazine articles and two books, *How to Avoid Housework* and *Guests Without Grief*.

Through it all, I've discovered that if I can control the mess around me, I can find serenity within, proving that even those of us whose DNA is predisposed to Dust, Neglect and Accumulation can rise above our gene pools and find domestic bliss.

The Plan

Cleaning and the Meaning of Life shows how to do just that. It's a divine plan that simplifies cleaning and boosts looks and livability, giving us the time, energy and spirit for the people and pursuits we love. It does so through my LIFE formula:

L—Lighten up

I—Invest in comfort

F—Forget perfection

E—Enhance flow

It's an easy way to take the mess out of domestic and the irk out of work with ideas that cost little or nothing to implement.

As a born-again neatnik (who occasionally slips), this simple formula has helped me and others avoid mess-induced stress—that out-of-control feeling generated by disarray and disorder. The LIFE plan also illustrates how to outwit dust and grime, create the illusion of clean, decorate with the major food group colors (at least until the kids are past the food-fight stage) and find heaven on earth at home.

Take Katie for instance. A stay-at-home mother of twins, a toddler and a hyperactive puppy, Katie wanted to regain control of her surroundings and find a measure of peace for herself. Keeping the LIFE formula in mind, I suggested she adopt a four-point strategy:

1. Pare down the family's glut of toys, clothing and equipment through rotation, donation and better storage.

2. Schedule a couple of timed clutter clearings a day.

3. Make the home *seem* cleaner and fresher by opening the windows to sunshine and fresh air anytime the weather allowed.

4. Create a "Mom Only" retreat.

Katie and I created her retreat by screening a corner of the master bedroom with ceiling-hung draperies and moving in a tweedy recliner, a soft cotton throw, a wall lamp, a fuzzy rug, a small reading table and an iPod. I also suggested she keep something fresh there, such as a pot of trailing philodendron or a vase of leafy branches from the magnolia outside her window. Snippets of nature are good for the soul.

Her retreat is off limits to papers, toys, and big and little visitors, making it a supremely serene decompression chamber that is effortless to maintain.

The Payoff

This simple approach has made a world of difference in Katie's life. Since her surroundings are now maintainable, she feels buoyed being in control of them. Plus her hideout (used when her husband, Joel, is in charge of the kids or when the kids are napping) has given her a measure of serenity she hasn't felt in years.

Sound good? It is. This book is my mission to minimize the daily grind and maximize the feel-good factors of home. I believe the more control we feel over our surroundings, the more content we feel inside. The more content we feel inside, the more joy we bring into our lives. The more joy we bring into our lives, the more joy we can bring into the lives of others. It's an all-encompassing circle for anyone who wants to rise above the dirty work and live a clean, serene and ultimately meaningful life.

Part I

Keeping the home trim is like keeping
the body toned. We get the best results cutting
excess at the source, staging small but frequent
workouts into big bloated piles and
knowing what, why and
how to let go.

Lighten Up

LIFE

CHAPTER ONE

TMS—
Too Much Stuff Syndrome

"Who is wealthy?
He who is content with what he has."

—The Talmud

It is the best of times. It is the worst of times. It is the age of information, but the deluge is drowning us. It is the season of want, but we're being buried alive. Most of us have much in the way of material goods but little in the way of time and contentment. All that is supposed to make us healthy, wealthy and wise is making us crazy and choking our lives.

In short, we're suffering from TMS—Too Much Stuff syndrome.

Some of the symptoms of TMS are similar to those of PMS: bloating, feeling out of sorts and an unusual craving for order. Sadly, TMS does or will affect most of us in

> "We want everything. We want it bigger, louder, shinier, faster, and we want it now. Instant gratification is as American as drive-through microwave apple pie."
>
> —Dennis Miller, comedian

our lifetimes and is only destined to worsen in our goods-driven society.

Life was free of TMS when home was a campfire in a snug cave, a few furs on the floor, maybe a nice hunting scene on the wall—the kind of artwork that stayed when we moved. But with progress came possessions; possessions that in time took on such importance, they followed us in death. Burial pits grew into mounds, mounds grew into chambers, chambers became the great pyramids that held more treasure for the future life than what was meant for the current one. Sort of like the self-storage units we rent today.

Today, we could give any pharaoh a run for his money with all the "treasures" we own. But it's gotten to the point, for many of us, where the treasures own us, not the other way around. Instead of enjoying life, we spend much of our time servicing what we do have or shopping for what we don't.

Sages through the ages have always known that owning more than we need weighs us down and compromises happiness. The Buddha warned his followers who coveted worldly goods, "Those who have cows have the care of cows." Jesus believed that we can't fully love one another when we're preoccupied with the acquisition of things. "Do not store up for yourselves treasure on earth, where it grows rusty and moth eaten," he cautioned. "For where your treasure is, there will be your heart." Taoism teaches that we can't live in the moment when we're burdened with possessions from the past. Its founder, Lao-tzu, summed up the secret to happiness when he pronounced, "He who knows he has enough is rich."

Even when we know we have enough, it's not always easy to let go. I know. I've held on to the excess much of my life. I grew up in a home that was so stuffed with stuff it was suffocating. Not good stuff, mind you, but dreck. Little was discarded because of the family motto, "We might need it someday." There was also "We paid good money for this," and the ever popular "This could be worth something at some point." That last motto could have been part of the family crest, if we had one. It would be inscribed under an illustration of baseball cards—the ones we could never find because on every horizontal surface sprawled layers of junk only a family of devout savers could hold onto.

> "Clutter doesn't just make it hard to close the doors on cupboards; it makes it hard to achieve closure in your life."
> —Dana Korey, professional organizer

The time we spent looking for things was mind-boggling, and trying to clean was a joke. Maintaining the place took twice as long as it should have, yet it always looked so messy it was embarrassing to have anyone over. We suffered from an acute case of TMS, and I longed to be free of it.

It was simple enough when I started my adult life with few belongings. But with marriage, two paychecks and then children, things started to mount, morph and take over. I had learned to take better care of things, but I knew we had too many things to take care of. That changed about five years ago, around the time I was living with the chaos of a whole house remodel and worrying about my daughter Lisa adventure racing in the mountains of Morocco.

It was a hot Saturday afternoon, the first day in months that we were free of contractors. I decided to take a dip in the pool, *au naturel*. I emerged from the water, naked as a newborn but a lot lumpier, when I saw *him*—an undetected painter staring down from the roof. Mortified, I sprinted across the patio into the house, ripping the tendon from my arch to my knee. The pain was so intense I could only stand for 20 minutes at a time, a condition that lasted nearly two years. Daily activities became a challenge, and shopping, an impossibility.

The lack of shopping was especially frustrating. I'd make these long lists of necessities for my family, the house and myself and fret because I couldn't get out to buy what I needed.

But then a funny thing happened. Weeks after I'd made the first list, I discovered I really didn't need or want most of what seemed so critical at the time. The hallway actually looked better without the rug I thought was so necessary, the missing earring magically materialized and I realized I would have worn those new brown boots that I coveted as much as the black ones that were already gathering cobwebs in my closet.

> "Simple is hard to do, but when you get there, it's so liberating."
>
> —Eileen Fisher, fashion designer

Now that I'm up and running again, the experience has put my acquisitiveness in perspective. I now know that I don't always need what I think I need, and most of the time I'm better off without it.

Like me, the most fervent followers of any doctrine are often converts. Take professional organizer Julie Morgenstern. This goddess of order confides that she spent the first quarter of her life in utter chaos. As an actress, director and artist, she was afraid she'd lose her creativity if she was held captive by systems and procedures, so she lived out of piles of stuff.

Her "aha!" moment came shortly after her daughter Jessie was born. "It was a beautiful spring day, and I wanted to take Jessie for her first walk," she said. "But it took me two and a half hours to find and pack what I believed I needed for her diaper bag. By the time I got it all together, she had fallen back to sleep. I thought, 'This child is not going to have a normal life if I don't get my act together.' I didn't want her to miss opportunities on my account. I had missed the moment."

It was a breakthrough. "I was willing to risk the creativity because I saw the reward on the other side of the piles," said Morgenstern, who now writes bestselling organizing books and an insightful column for *O* magazine.

I never considered the connection between chaos and my own creativity; I just knew too much stuff was draining me of too much time and energy, two things I never seemed to have enough of. In my own quest for the cure, I've learned more than a few tricks about the judicious buying, purging and organizing of things, which I've detailed in the following chapters. These are small, affordable, easy-to-implement ideas that have made a huge difference in the quality of my life. What I've learned can improve your life, too.

Recognize the
Seven Warning Signs of TMS

Most of us suffer in some degree from TMS. Learn how serious your case is from the following symptoms:

1. **Bloating**—Whether it's overcrowded bookshelves, closets or cabinets, clutter not only causes discomfort, it adds ugly pounds and bulges.
2. **Headache**—The responsibility of insuring, storing and caring for too many things can bring on many a migraine.
3. **Supersensitivity**—"You love your *Playboy* collection more than you love me. Admit it."
4. **Cravings**—"I know I stashed those Snickers bars somewhere in the freezer, but they've disappeared amid the frostbitten mystery meats."

5. **Fatigue**—How much more energy would we have if there were fewer items to move, sort and clean?

6. **Cramps**—Who doesn't get pangs and spasms from moving that stuff around every time we need a clear space to eat, work or sleep?

7. **Moodiness**—"How can I possibly (sob) give that presentation if I can't find my lucky panties or my notes?"

Diagnosis:

1–3 symptoms: Congratulations! You're in great health. Be sure to stay that way by continuing to practice "all things in moderation."

4–6 symptoms: It might be wise to lay off the flea markets, the mall and eBay for a while. Consider monthly clutter colonics instead.

7 symptoms: You suffer from a full-blown case of affluenza. Give your charge card a rest, crawl under the covers and read the following chapters.

What We Gain from Living with Less

❀ **Time** is the biggest bonus—it's what we need to enjoy life's great gifts: family, friends and the great outdoors. When there's less stuff to fuss with, there are more hours to play with.

❀ **Energy** is another perk—it's the essential fuel we need to pursue our passions, whether they involve travel, sports or romance. Too many possessions drain that energy.

❀ **Serenity** also comes into play—when we learn to live with less, there's less mess-induced stress. There is also less worry about the care, loss or insurance of things.

> "If there is to be any peace, it will come through being, not having."
>
> —Henry Miller, writer

Space? The less stuff we have, the bigger our surroundings feel and the better they flow. As New York interior designer Clodagh writes in *Total Design,* "A feeling of spaciousness is determined far more by clarity and energy flow than by square feet."

Other benefits from living a pared life:

- **Focus:** The home is like the mind. It works best when it's clear of brain-boggling clutter.

- **Spontaneity:** When we don't have a pile of possessions tying us down, we're more open to spur-of-the-moment outings and long-term travel.

> "There must be more to life than having everything."
>
> —Maurice Sendak, writer

- **Charisma:** When we're consumed with shopping for, maintaining and discussing our possessions, we become shallow and boring. By taming an acquisitive lifestyle, we open our minds and our hearts to more interesting pursuits and thus attract more interesting people.

- **A Richer Life:** It's simple math: If we spend less, we save more. Besides, what's going to comfort us in the end is not the stuff we've hoarded but the love we've given away.

LIFE MATTERS:

The Ransom of Possessions

Rich and Sue are down-to-earth teachers who used to love hosting end-of-the year parent/student potlucks and inviting friends over to shoot pool and watch videos, at least until they got "lucky." That's when Sue inherited a bundle of money and a bulging houseful of objects from her wealthy art dealer uncle.

The couple liked their old tract home, but since it was way too small and seemed unworthy of show-casing their new possessions, they put the windfall into a larger, more elegant place. Sumptuous fabrics, handwoven rugs and French limestone floors are now a backdrop to the precious art and antiques that fill each room. The effect is stunning but so pre-cious, it's put a crimp in their former open-house policy. They've become understandably paranoid about anyone dribbling on the white silk sofas or marring the eighteenth-century walnut tables. So the school and the billiard parties are in the past. In their place, one gets a house tour. The offer of a drink or a nibble? Fahhgedaboutit—they might leave their mark. The couple now lives in a gilded cage, prisoners of their own possessions.

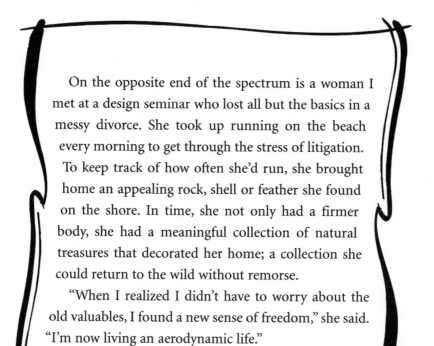

On the opposite end of the spectrum is a woman I met at a design seminar who lost all but the basics in a messy divorce. She took up running on the beach every morning to get through the stress of litigation. To keep track of how often she'd run, she brought home an appealing rock, shell or feather she found on the shore. In time, she not only had a firmer body, she had a meaningful collection of natural treasures that decorated her home; a collection she could return to the wild without remorse.

"When I realized I didn't have to worry about the old valuables, I found a new sense of freedom," she said. "I'm now living an aerodynamic life."

CHAPTER TWO

The Art of Letting Go

"You shouldn't go through life with a catcher's mitt on both hands; you need to be able to throw some things back."

—Maya Angelou, writer

Nothing was ever let go at Calke Abbey. The circa 1701 country house in Derbyshire, England, was, until recently, filled to the gills with centuries of clothing, furniture, toys, stuffed birds and reptiles, papers and other possessions. Each generation of the family who owned the immense manor simply closed the doors on the previous generation's debris and moved to another set of rooms.

One family member even stashed away his wife. The reclusive Sir Henry Harpur married a lady's maid then hid her away so no man could gaze upon her beauty. Eventually, he built secret passageways and a tunnel through the garden so he too could not be seen.

Whether all that hoarded stuff led to eccentric behavior or the behavior led to the hoarding of stuff is anyone's guess. But haven't you ever wanted to close the door on clutter and move on? I know I have. Yet when I move, I tend to take it all with me.

> "Clutter is the root of all evil."
>
> —Louise Rafkin,
> *Other People's Dirt*

Years ago, my airline pilot husband, Larry, was transferred to San Diego, our base of choice. So, along with our two young daughters, Kelley and Lisa, we packed up everything we owned, moved it across the country, put it in storage and rented a furnished house for eighteen months. It was one of the best times of our lives. We suddenly had time to go to the beach, play tennis, socialize, read—all the things we love to do. In addition, Larry became a youth soccer coach, and I went back to school. But despite feeling light and free, I wanted my things. I longed for my green velvet sofa, my own pots and pans, my rugs, my decorative pillows, throws, linens, pictures, papers and doll collection.

When we moved into the new house and finally unpacked our stuff, I couldn't believe what I had missed: a huge collection of mostly motley goods. It was like reconnecting with a high school sweetheart; the reality didn't live up to the memory.

Did we get rid of this old stuff? Naw. Since the new house we finally moved into was bigger, we just kept adding layers of matter: furnishings, toys, small appliances, china, electronics, you-name-it. Everything purchased was with an eye toward improving our lives. That was the promise. The reality was quite different, though it took me years to see it. Just about everything needed space, cleaning, repair, tracking, manuals, insurance and so on. Eventually, there just wasn't the time or energy to do all the things we, or at least I (since I'm the primary caretaker) wanted to do.

It took a remodeling of the house years later for me to see the light. Once again, Larry and I had to clear out and live with only the necessities, but this time in the reduced space of three small rooms.

The kids were out on their own, so we whittled down to the bare bones in our makeshift laundry room-kitchen, where meal preparation was simple and cleanup a snap. Two sets of towels worked in the bathroom, and since we wore only what we could pack in two suitcases, laundry loads lessened. And with no TV and little in the bedroom except a big bed to collapse into, we talked, read and fell

> "A house is just a pile of stuff with a cover on it. . . . And even though you might like your house, you gotta move. Gotta get a bigger house. Why? Too much stuff!"
>
> —George Carlin, comedian

asleep early. I'm not saying it was bliss, but it taught us how little we really need and how having little freed our time and brought us closer.

Rooms have filled again, but sparsely this time. I made a list of what's important in my life and, in so doing, was able to chuck all that didn't enhance and further those pursuits. For instance, I know I'll never be a decent gardener, so I've donated all my gardening books, seed packets and other growing paraphernalia that I've amassed over the years and made the yard as low maintenance as possible. When I realized I didn't need dolls to remind me of my travels (I bought one in every place I visited), I donated that collection as well.

> "You don't need a thing to hold onto a feeling."
>
> —Don Aslett
> *Office Clutter Cure*

I rid us of a ton of trappings before the remodel, and I continue to prune on a more or less regular basis. I now know that every item I bring into the house will demand something of me, and everything I eliminate means one less thing that takes up my time and space.

If you'd like more time and space and less stress in your life, and you lack a spare manor where you can stash the excess, give some thought to letting go. Here are some thoughts on doing so.

The Path to En-Lighten-Ment

❀ **Where am I now?** Figure out what you want at this stage in life. The focus might be on losing weight, landing a more satisfying job or spending more time with the family. Whatever it is, when you focus on the path, you can better chuck the rubble that gets in the way. When writer Danielle Brown had her first baby, she was subscribing to a half dozen magazines and a couple of newspapers. "I suddenly had no time to read, and those stacks kept growing," she said. "They became tyrants before I had the courage to chuck them and cancel the subscriptions."

> "Life is constant change. So when something comes into your life enjoy it, use it well, and when it is time, let it go."
>
> —Karen Kingston,
> *Clear Your Clutter with Feng Shui*

❀ **Why is it hard to toss some things and not others?** I could chuck my own clothes with ease, but I saved so much of my kids' infant apparel, I could have opened a baby boutique. It wasn't just because those tiny smocked dresses and embroidered bibs were so cute, it was because it was hard to see my girls grow up. Once I figured that saving their things wasn't going to slow the process, I could finally give it all away.

❀ **What can I toss that's slowing me down?** Exercise equipment that only gathers cobwebs begets guilt. Superfluous toiletries that have to be pawed through keep us from the good stuff. Book clubs that generate an avalanche of paperwork add dead weight and make life's journey a slog.

❀ **The more we have, the less we use.** A closet full of clothes with nothing to wear is a common complaint for many of us, and providing a roomful of playthings makes kids so over-whelmed they can't focus on any one thing for long. As family psychologist and author John Rosemond maintains, the more toys a child has, the less able he is to enter-tain himself.

> "The more you know, the less you need."
>
> —Australian aboriginal proverb

❀ **Live for today.** I know a woman whose home is stuffed with the furnishings from both her own home and her late parents' home. She knows her rooms are crowded and dreary, but she says every item reminds her of better days. Ironically, she's stuck in a dead-end job and a stagnant relationship. It's as if her possessions have kept her in a permanent state of childhood.

❀ **Take time to give thanks for life's blessings.** When we focus on the spiritual, the materialistic takes on less importance.

Prepare for Purge-Atory

❀ **Get ready.** The night before the purge, set up everything you need: a large trash can for dumping, recycling bins, boxes and bags for the donation and sale of stuff, markers and labels and clear plastic boxes for the treasures to be saved. If you'll be working on a dark corner or closet, move a floor lamp to the area. A job begun is a job half done. Well, almost.

❀ **Take before-and-after shots of the offending area before starting.** I find tacking both photos on the inside of my closet door helps motivate me to keep the area tidier and gives me a tangible sense of satisfaction when I am done.

> "Once you've taken that critical step of editing down, your home can be a place to relax, instead of a reminder of all that's to be done."
>
> —Kim Johnson Gross,
> *Chic Simple*

❀ **Decide ahead how much time to allot to paring down.** Set up a kitchen timer to stay on track. A ticking timer is a great audio and visual motivator.

❀ **Know that the process may be long and hard.** When consummate collector Barbara Kaufman purged her bedroom closet to make room for a California Closets system of bins, bells and whistles, the operation took a full five weeks: two weeks for her to remove and pile huge quantities of stuff in another room, three days for the actual installation, two weeks for the "psychiatric discarding process" and almost another week to put it all back. "It has changed things for me," said Barbara. "Everything has its own tidy place, and I now know where to find it all."

❧ **Clutter control is an ongoing challenge.** Rather than staging one all-out attack, make clutter control a regular encounter. Interior designer and author Alexandra Stoddard launches monthly clutter clearing sessions at work and weekly ones at home. "A regular, serious attack on mess and unnecessary clutter, performed with a glad heart, makes you feel in control of all the parts of your life you care about," she writes in *Living a Beautiful Life*.

> "If you want to move a mountain, you need to start by carrying away the stones."
> —Chinese proverb

> "To have more, desire less."
> —*Table Talk*

❧ **Make decisions now, not later.** Keeping stuff in limbo won't open the gates to clutter-free paradise.

Make a Purge a Piece of Cake

⚖ **Start on a prime spot.** Greeted with chronically messy shelves every time you drive into the garage? You'll get more bang for the buck by putting your energies there rather than in a more remote corner. The same goes for closets. The condition of the master bedroom closet is directly related to how quick the morning getaway is, so its order is more critical than the one down the hall.

⚖ **Break a big job into small segments.** A month of 30-minute garage-clearing sessions every Saturday morning puts a doable dent in debris.

⤵ **Be realistic about how much time a particular area takes to tackle so you won't have to leave it in shambles.** I once broke down my main closet into towering heaps of clothes before I realized I had more important things to attend to. I lived out of those piles for weeks before I could take the time to cull and organize them. I looked rumpled for weeks from the wrinkles.

⤵ **Never schedule more than a couple of hours for a purge or you'll burn out.** Besides, short spurts are more apt to get you into a tossing habit.

⤵ **Trash the largest items first from a heap of clutter.** It reduces the pile faster, which is always encouraging.

⤵ **Schedule a visit from a charity that picks up items or place them in your car and take them to Goodwill or wherever else they're headed.** Just don't wait too long, or those items will take root in the trunk.

> "Art is the elimination of the unnecessary."
> —Pablo Picasso

The Procrastinator's Guide to Letting Go

I'd rather read, nap, walk, cook and submit the tenderest parts of my body to electrolysis than deal with a heap on my desk or a disheveled closet. When stuff gets out of hand, I've been known to play the following tricks on myself.

✿ **Plan a party in a month or so.** There's nothing like peer pressure to get the place whipped into shape.

✿ **Invite a houseguest.** Knowing that someone, especially a neatnik-in-law, is peering into my unruly medicine cabinet or scrutinizing my collection of ratty linens is sure to get me in a tossing mood.

❀ **Schedule a Goodwill or Salvation Army pickup within the week.** The thought of a scowling, empty-handed pickup crew always motivates me to fill boxes.

❀ **Start sorting something I love but have neglected, like that drawer of tangled costume jewelry or a vast collection of photos.** I find it almost, but not quite,  fun to cull and organize the things I like best.

❀ **Visit a model home.** I have been known to fantasize that I could actually live such an ordered, detritus-free existence. Before I snap out of it, I start chucking.

❀ **Reward myself after a clearing.** My rewards include a walk on the beach, a good read over a mocha latte in my favorite café, a professional manicure (I usually need it after a major purge), a long candlelit bath (I usually need that, too). Anything enjoyable works, as long as it doesn't generate more stuff.

❀ **Turn it into a ritual.** In many cultures, the last day of the year is the traditional time to clear out the old. Icelanders burn a glut of goods in big bonfires; Neapolitans toss old plates, pots and pans out the window; and Scots make it a point to clear all debts before midnight. I've long saved the day to clear out every last vestige of Christmas and then some.

❀ **Remind myself that clutter is the child of indecision and procrastination.** And I have neither the time nor the patience to raise another child.

Separation Anxiety

When things take root, they seem to become a part of who we are, so it's not always easy to let go. Here are some ways to make the sweet sorrow of parting easier.

> "When you get down to it, it's surprising how little we need to be happy."
> —Elaine St. James, *Inner Simplicity*

- ✿ **Cut it out.** Clothes, especially those with sentimental value, can be some of the hardest things to release. That cheerleading uniform from high school, the suede mini you wore when you met your mate, the bridesmaid's dress from your best friend's wedding all beg to be kept. But honestly, how often do we drag saved clothes out of storage and swoon over them? Give into sentiment and practicality by cutting a square of the fabric from treasured items to make a collage, a chair cushion, a pillow or a quilt. Toss the rest. No time or talent for sewing? Hand over the project to a tailor.

- ✿ **Renounce martyrdom.** Inherited furnishings are tough to part with, but they can also be some of the worst things to live with. In her book *Simple Abundance,* Sarah Ban Breathnach tells of inheriting two huge and hideous lamps that she lived with for fifteen years before she sent them packing. "Every time I came into the living room, I found myself recoiling from these lamps," she wrote. "Finally one day, God's interior decorator said in desperation, 'Well, get rid of the damn things and stop whining.'"

> "It's harder to unburden possessions than it is to buy them."
> —Clodagh, interior designer

❀ **Find the profit in the loss.** Understand that the act of parting can be painful, especially for long-held stuff. "I've discarded some things that I've saved," said Barbara Kaufman, a collector of everything from miniature boxes to old shopping bags. "The decision making was difficult, but when it was over, I felt lighter and freer and did not pine for the departed."

> "Learn to let go. That is the key to happiness."
>
> —The Buddha

THE RUBBISH INQUISITION: FIVE QUESTIONS TO PONDER

1. If there were a fire or flood, would I try to save this?

2. Would I pay a mover to move it?

3. Does it make my life easier?

4. Does it make me or my surroundings look better?

5. Would I be able to find it if I needed it again?

LIFE MATTERS:

Love after Litter

*H*ey, it can happen. The former president of the Los Angeles branch of Clutterer's Anonymous admitted that his house was once so littered, it looked like it had been ransacked. And that was *before* the place was burglarized.

The investigating police officer remarked, "Boy, they really made a mess here."

"They hadn't," said Larry, who retains his anonymity by divulging only his first name. "It was my mess."

He says that moment was a turning point in his battle against clutter. He confesses that it's a constant struggle, since he believes he has a stronger attachment to things than most people. But he knew he had turned a corner when he discarded the photographs, furnishings and other reminders of a former but significant relationship.

The next week, he met and fell in love with his future spouse.

"Some may see that as a result of having no strings attached," he said. "But some of us call it the 'Woo-Woo Factor.' Because I let something go, a vacuum was created, and something else came in to fill it."

Worthy Places to Donate

We can always take photos of the good stuff, register and sell it on eBay or go the consignment shop or garage sale route, but donating stuff is good karma. My aesthetician-friend Eileen Tichenor Doak claims the better the stuff, the better the karma. It's a case of share and the world shares with you; horde and you horde alone.

> "It is more blessed to give than to receive."
> —Acts 20:35

To find a worthy organization that's glad to get your goods and give you the karma of a tax write-off, check the IRS Web site *(www.IRS.gov)* or call IRS customer service at 877-829-5500.

Three Things to Remember About Donating Goods

1. **If you're unsure whether an organization can use a particular castoff, call before hauling it over.**

2. **If an item is large and unwieldy, like a sofa or a bed, ask if it can be retrieved.** Many of the larger nonprofits offer pickup service.

3. **Don't donate junk.** The charity will have to discard it anyway, so you're just wasting their time and money. I knew an elegant woman who would cut the buttons from every designer piece of clothing she bestowed to our church's thrift shop. Unfortunately for the sorters, of which I was one, most everything she donated had to be dumped.

What to Dump

The following can't be donated or, in most cases, recycled, so it's always best to chuck.

- ❀ **UFOs.** If you can't recognize an unidentifiable freezer object now, another layer of frost isn't going to help, and it's not going to improve with age.

- ❀ **Bedraggled houseplants that beg for a mercy killing.**

- ❀ **Fuzzy toilet seat covers.** They may warm the buns, but they attract germs and add to the laundry load.

- ❀ **Toiletries and cosmetics that have changed color, consistency or smell.** These breeders of bacteria not only make it harder to find the good stuff, too many on a counter make cleaning a hassle.

> "The wisdom of life consists of the elimination of nonessentials."
>
> —Lin Yutang, philosopher

- ❀ **Unfixable anything.**

- ❀ **Anything that has accumulated a thick layer of "don't use it enough" dust.**

- ❀ **Old grudges.** "To err is human, to forgive is divine." Go for divine.

> "Grace fills empty spaces, but it can only enter where there is a void to receive it."
>
> —Simone Weil, *Gravity and Grace*

What to Keep

People and possessions that make you feel good, function better and add to the quality of your life.

CHAPTER THREE

Beat the Paper Beast

*"What the world really needs is more
love and less paperwork."*

—Pearl Bailey

Listen. Can you hear it? It's the rustle of junk mail creeping into the mailbox, the thump of the newspaper hitting the porch, the rattle of school papers being hauled off the bus. The sound may be subtle, but it's insidious. It's a sign that a blood-sucking beast is about to take over your desk, your counters, your tables and your time. For you can't just chuck paper; you have to read it, sort it, file it, pay it and ponder it before it makes its way out the door. *If* it makes its way out the door.

We can't actually obliterate this beast, but we can make it behave.

Minimize Mega Mail

I used to pick up my friend Liz's mail when she traveled, which was much of the time. Because she's the queen of catalog shopping, she'd get a gazillion of the things, which generated yet more mail since her name seemed to be sold to every other outfit in the country. Fed up with the glut and unwilling to give either of us a hernia, she took action by writing to the Direct Mail Association, instructing it to remove her name from its member mailing lists.

A year after registering with the DMA, she figures her junk mail has been cut at least in half. "I still get the catalogs I want," she said. "But I no longer get all those credit card offers and the rest of that superfluous crap."

"Beauty magazines make you feel ugly."
—Kelley Jhung

The DMA is a trade association of national advertisers who are legally bound to keep names off their mailing lists for five years when instructed to do so. At the end of the five-year period, you have to reregister to stay off the lists. How can you remember in five years? That new truckload of mail will tell you.

If you want to lighten that load now, contact

Mail Preference Service
Direct Marketing Association
P.O. Box 643
Carmel, NY 10512
212-768-7277

Mail registration is free, or for $5.00, you can register online at *www.the-dma.org.*

The DMA says it represents 75 percent of national advertisers. For the rest, as well as for local advertisers and political mailings, here are some ways to stem the flow.

➴ Create and save a form letter on the computer requesting your removal from a mailing list. Send it to any company that overdoes the correspondence.

≥ Instruct the phone company to remove your address from the next phone book so local mail solicitors can't track you down.

≥ Send your own change of address cards instead of using the U.S. Post Office's. It seems even the postal service wants to make a buck off our names by putting them up for grabs.

≥ Question dealings with any business that generates deep drifts of mail. I gave up ordering books through book clubs long ago partly because they buried me in such an avalanche of advertising, I had no time to read the books I ordered.

≥ If you enter the house via the garage or building lobby, dump the junk in the recycling bin or trash can before it sullies the inner sanctum.

Housebreak Newspapers

Newspapers are another mess-making time tyrant, especially the Sunday paper, which spreads itself all over the house in the hours it takes to plow through. I'm still hooked on reading mine, but I'm currently considering the following alternatives:

> "Spend your time reading, not feeling guilty over what you haven't read."
>
> —Barbara Hemphill,
> *Taming the Paper Tiger*

❀ **Read the online version.** Just about every major newspaper in the country, including *The New York Times*, *USA Today* and the *Los Angeles Times*, has a free Internet offering that won't litter the living room, overwhelm the reader or clog the recycling bin. *Let Go of Clutter* author, Harriet Schechter,

 accesses a wide range of news by reading a slew of national and regional papers online. "There are so many advantages to the online version," said the organizing expert. "I can read more stories in less time, I can easily share relevant articles via e-mail and I no longer have inky fingers."

🌼 **Read someone else's paper.** I had a neighbor who walked a mile and a half every morning to breakfast and a perusal of the café's many newspapers, keeping his body slim and his home trim. No time to walk? Consider sharing a subscription with a close neighbor.

🌼 **Turn on the tube.** It's hard to chop veggies or boil a pot of pasta while perusing the paper, but it's a natural inclination when watching Peter Jennings or Bill O'Reilly.

🌼 **If you can't give up getting the paper, at least give up saving it.** My mother held onto months of the *Boston Globe* and the *Quincy Patriot Ledger* "to read and clip later." Later rarely came, and our den, where the papers were stored, looked like a newspaper distribution center after an earthquake. Only messier.

"It's the too much information age."
—Kathleen Squires, writer

Control Photos

Ask anyone what they'd most likely save in a fire. Nine times out of ten, it's their collection of family photographs. Twice my family has had to evacuate our home when a Southern California fire threatened, and twice the photos were the first things we grabbed. The experience taught me to keep our collection edited to a manageable level and stored so that it's accessible, mobile and safe. Here are some ways to manage your photos:

- ⚓ **Toss unflattering pictures immediately.** I've learned to secretly wrap any shot that makes me look fat or ugly in a piece of trash so no one sees it and says, "You're tossing this? The dog looks great!"

- ⚓ **Dump the double.** If it's not slated for friend or family, what's the point?

- ⚓ **Compile a collection of photos on a personal CD or DVD.**  Most photo processing labs can transfer 100 or so shots onto one slim disc for under $10. Family Tree Video in San Diego typically transfers around 500 photos into story form onto a disc, incorporating home movies, favorite music and special effects. "We actually can fit more photos, but it's a more interesting product if shots are trimmed to under 500," said spokesman John Snyder.

COVER GIRLS

My husband, sentimental guy that he is, has found a unique way of enjoying family photos. He's glued his favorites on the covers of the manila folders in his files, so when he pulls a file on taxes or insurance, there is at least one of his girls smiling back at him.

- ⚓ **Always have an empty photo album on hand.** Being an album ahead means we're less apt to toss photos in a drawer to deal with later . . . or not. Small albums are especially good for individual events like a party or a trip and are less intimidating to fill. They're also more portable.

THE PICTURE OF GUILT

Don't feel guilty if your photos are in shoeboxes. They're out of damaging sunlight and are easy to flip through, provided there's flippin' room. However, it's a good idea to invest in a few archival quality acid- and lignin-free photo boxes, since common cardboard may deteriorate photos over time.

The Beauty and Bane of Books

Books are wondrous things. Not only do they inform and entertain, a bookcase full of them insulates, soundproofs and adds character to a room. I'm a hard-core book hoarder, but when I reach the point when there are more books than there are shelves, a little action is in order.

> "You must say 'no' to some things in order to say 'yes' to reading."
> —Susan Richmond, *The Toastmaster*

- Think of the town library as a treasure house of reading material. Sign up for a library card, and you won't ever need to buy, store or dust Stephen King or Jane Austen again.

- Guidebooks are rarely good for more than a year since restaurants go out of business, hotels change hands, and prices and new attractions open. Instead of hauling a guidebook back home, leave it in the hotel lobby for an incoming visitor.

- Become a "Book Crosser" and let your just-read book have an adventure. A Book Crosser is someone who intentionally leaves books for others in public places like coffee shops, park benches and airport lounges. They can then track the book's travels on the Internet. BookCrossing *(www.bookcrossing.com)* is a free global book club that fosters literacy, generosity and uncrammed bookcases. Register your latest just-read book at the Web site, add a message about the book and yourself, and then release the book into the wild. With any luck, the finder will read the book, log onto the Web site, add his or her message and pass the book along in a similar manner. Think of it as literary karma.

> "A book is not only a friend, it makes friends for you. When you have possessed a book with mind and spirit, you are enriched. But when you pass it on you are enriched threefold."
>
> —Henry Miller, *The Books in My Life*

❀ Pare bedside reading matter. Reading in bed is one of life's great pleasures, but since we can only peruse one book or magazine at a time, it's best to limit our choices to one or two publications.

❀ Photocopy favorite recipes from dated cookbooks then donate the books to a library book sale.

❀ Never waste time reading a boring book. If it doesn't grab you by the first two chapters, chances are it's not going to grab you at all. "There's no thief like a bad book," says the Italian proverb.

De-Stress Your Desk

The eye may adjust to seeing piles of paper on a desk, but the psyche stresses over it. I used to pile every bill, catalog and paper-to-be-filed on my desk until it was a mind-muddling mess. I tried

> "Creativity languishes on the cluttered desktop."
> —Kathryn Collins,
> *The Western Guide to Feng Shui*

to get organized by tossing papers in a big boot-box, which I covered with pretty adhesive paper, but because I had to actually lift the lid, papers would land on top of it instead of in it. I've since cleared out a junk drawer that's now designated to accept anything that needs weekly attention. There is still the errant paper or two (or three or four) on my desktop, but there are no longer messy mounds of them. A few other ideas:

- Challenge yourself to dump as much paper as possible into the wastebasket *before* it hits your desk. The neatest desks are often the result of the fullest wastebaskets.

- Most of us are multitaskers, but it helps to have only one undertaking at a time on a desk. Don Aslett, author and king of clutter control, says that he may have thirty projects going at once, but he only keeps one of them on his desk so he can fully focus on it until it's done.

- Make paperwork more tolerable by buying office supplies at an art supply store. I find little things like round stainless steel paperclips and neon sticky notes take some of the tedium out of deskwork. Also, invest in a good pen. "One beautifully crafted pen that feels just right in your hand is better than a fistful of Bics," believes interior designer Clodagh.

- Recipe clippings are notorious desk hoggers, so it helps to have a clipping criterion. My criteria are healthy ingredients, a minimum of them and simple, easy-to-follow steps. Even then, I clip more than I cook, but I keep untried recipes down to a manageable mound by striving to try one new dish a week.

⚖ Organize papers for a temporary project, like a wedding or a remodel, in a portable accordion file so info is organized and ready to travel when needed.

⚖ If the dining table functions as the family desk most of the time, consider using the drawers and shelves of surrounding furniture for files, reference books and office supplies. When I needed to set up an office in the dining room of a furnished rental years ago, I transformed the china cabinet into an office organizer, screening supplies with shirred curtains mounted behind the glass doors.

⚖ Make peace with your piles. Not apt to file away at the end of the day? Join the club and stack things instead. Paper piles aren't so bad if they're *neat* paper piles. Even if they're not, you can always turn them into abstract sculptures by draping them with silk scarves.

> "If you are searching for the perfect organizing solution, be assured that none exists."
>
> —Julie Morgenstern, *Organizing from the Inside Out*

FIVE FREQUENT FILER POINTS

1. Buy quality cabinets. I once owned some "bargain" cabinets that had drawers that stuck and metal support frames that kept collapsing. Filing procrastination became a way of life for me.

2. Get in the habit of filing papers either in the very front or very back of a folder so you can reach the latest entry easily.

3. Use staples instead of paperclips. Paperclips have a way of latching onto other papers—usually the elusive ones we're looking for.

4. Make it a point to toss at least one dated or extraneous paper each time you flip through a file.

5. Rethink filing. Binders are sometimes better than files since they better organize a mass of material. I keep three-ring binders for Christmas lists, menus and craft ideas. I also have a binder of financial and insurance info, as well as one for future decorating projects.

Simplify Bill Paying

❀ Scale down to one credit card. The fewer the bills, the less the paperwork.

❀ Eliminate late fees, stamps, envelopes and fuss by setting up an  automatic bill paying account through your bank for regular bills like utilities, insurance premiums and loans. Or pay bills online with Quicken or Microsoft Money software or through *www.transpoint.com*. I figure I save at least a weekly half hour of work and a half pound of hassles since I started paying many of my bills this way.

❀ Make it a point to deal with bills at least twice a month. Frequent little nibbles prevent big bloated piles. They also prevent sky-high interest fees.

❀ Whether it's in a walnut-paneled den or a cement block corner of the basement, make the bill-paying station as pleasant as possible with a comfortable chair, good lighting and a fresh flower or live plant to lighten a burdensome job.

DON'T BURY GRANNY

Need a motivating force to keep your desktop clear? Arrange a photo collage of family, friends and pets on it, and top it with a cut-to-fit piece of glass. Few of us can keep those we love hidden for long.

Bits and Pieces

✂ Rather than holding onto ticket stubs, programs and such, keep a journal. Our thoughts and feelings about an event are more meaningful over time than yellowing bits of this and that.

✂ Cultivate decision-making skills early in life by having children select what is to be displayed, sent to Grandma, made into wrapping paper or released into the recycling bin. The sooner one learns to cull and organize, the more ingrained it becomes. The more ingrained it becomes, the more it influences other areas of life.

Design for Living

A Cooler Fridge

As a one-time photo stylist for a decorating magazine, I've seen some of the prettiest kitchens gunked up by a thick crust of messages, mail, cartoons, photos, school papers, what-have-you on the refrigerator door.

It's easy to undress the mess by creating a message center on the inside of a kitchen cabinet door, using chalkboard paint, a metallic bulletin board or even blue painter's tape.

What about all those masterpieces from your mini-Monet? One woman I know has the copy shop shrink them down to three-ring binder size, slips them into plastic page protectors and displays "The Portfolio" on the coffee table.

"I have one for each child," said Dallas art teacher Denise McCoy. "They love flipping through them with their friends," she said. "And I love having a clear fridge door."

LIFE MATTERS:

What Would You Save?

A fire is raging in the nearby woods. The big dam upstream is about to break. Ten-foot waves are crashing over the nearby seawall.

Quick, after the family and pets are accounted for, what would you save if your home were threatened by disaster and you had only ten minutes to evacuate? Family photos? Insurance papers? Love letters? Make a list of can't-live-without items and post it somewhere obvious.

Better to plan in the calm of normalcy than in the panic of flight.

CHAPTER FOUR

Curb the Shopping Urge

"The money you spend today you might remake tomorrow, but the time you spend spending can never be bought back."

—William Safire, columnist,
The New York Times

It's out there somewhere. I just know it. That perfect outfit that's going to nip my waist, lift my bottom and make me look and feel like I could knock 'em dead. It will not only be totally flattering, it will pull together every mismatched piece already hanging in my bulging closet.

How many hours have I spent hunting for this Holy Grail? Oh, probably about as many as it would take to earn a doctorate, train for a triathlon *and* find a cure for world hunger. That's not even counting the hours I've put in shopping for cosmetics, gadgets and other things that

"A saleslady holds up an ugly dress and says, 'This looks so much better on.' On what? On fire?"

—Rita Rudner, comedian

promised to save me time and improve my life but just seemed to complicate it.

It is time to face the truth: Recreational shopping not only makes me lust for what I lack, it's expensive, time consuming, energy draining and, in the end, a pretty empty way to spend the day. Worse, it's a major source of clutter and work, since everything purchased takes up space and demands maintenance.

"I know people who buy for the sake of buying, always newer, always better, always more, never enough."

—Linda Ligon,
Natural Home magazine

But it's not easy to resist the call of the mall. Even when I'm not actively looking for that perfect thing, I find it soothing to be someplace where I can fondle the cashmere, hear the tinkling of a live piano and smell exotic blends of expensive perfumes.

Apparently, I'm not alone. In the comic strip *Cathy*, its creator, Cathy Guisewite, has her heroine justify her hard-core shopping habit by explaining, "I just want to be someplace where the clothes are ironed, the dishes are all clean and everything else is stacked neatly on a nice, dusted shelf."

That can be reason enough for a cartoon character, but I figured if I wanted more time in my life for what counts, my shopping habits would have to be reprogrammed. But how? That answer came once I realized that my *need* (and, I suspect, the need of many others) for something tangible is often the least motivating factor for hitting the mall, and that there may be a more satisfying substitute for shopping.

Next time you get the impulse to cruise and peruse the shops, stop to consider why. Sometimes we shop because we like the personal service and the pristine order of our favorite store. Can that feeling be better served by splurging on a professional house cleaning? Or maybe it's the sensory feel of luxurious fabrics and fragrant lotions that lure us in the door. Perhaps a scented soak in a bubbling bath would better appease that need. For many of us, the shopping drive simply springs from the universal desire to look better. I can often meet that need with a home facial or a pedicure or, better yet, a new hairstyle. I've also been known to have my eyelashes professionally curled and dyed. I find salon curled and tinted lashes the best thing since Botox and a lot cheaper. The dye lasts about a month and the curl about three months. I always have both done before a trip so I can simplify my makeup on the road and look half-decent when I wake in the morning. Dark, curled and natural-looking lashes perk me up more than any new outfit.

> "The thrill was in the trying on, in the buying. The moment after she had acquired something new, it became meaningless to her."
>
> —Judith Krantz, *Scruples*

The Seduction of Shopping

I've found one of the easiest ways to tame my shopping habit is to let my list marinate for at least a couple of weeks before I buy anything on it. I know I probably either have a good substitute or don't really need it. It's not that the urge isn't there, but I've learned to control it better.

I've also learned a few other disciplines along the way. Taming my TV habit, for one. When we're bombarded with images that promise a happier, sexier and more fulfilled life, we naturally want to run out and buy, or dial up and order, whatever it takes to have that life. Truth is, the fewer commercials we're exposed to, the more content we are with what we have. Watch less, want less.

Canceling catalogs and unregistering for Internet notices also helps control the urge to splurge. It can also save a bundle of time and trouble. The hours I've spent poring over catalogs and Web pages, waiting for merchandise, then repacking, paying for postage and standing in line to return all that didn't fit, didn't flatter or was downright ugly, I could have better spent loitering in a real store.

Yet it's impossible to completely avoid the seductive lure of advertising. "Marketers have gotten so good at making products attractive and accessible that it's hard to resist even the things we have no use for," maintains Irene Tobis of Ducks-in-a-Row Efficiency Consultants in Madison, Wisconsin. "But it's a lot like alcoholism," said the psychologist. "You can remove yourself from the problem."

Here are a few other truths to keep in mind:

> "We used to build civilizations. Now we build shopping centers."
> —Bill Bryson, writer

- ❀ **Lures can be limited.** Rather than making a special trip to the home center or mall to pick up a set of potholders, dish towels or some other domestic necessity, buy them during your weekly shopping at the supermarket. At the grocery store, we're not likely to be seduced by that new bed-in-a-bag set or the latest latte maker, and we can often take care of dry cleaning, photo processing and banking to boot.

- ❀ **High maintenance is the road to low usage.** How often do we reach for that pink silk jacket or those white wool pants when we know they're a magnet for stains and a generator of dry-cleaning bills? I once owned a beaded top whose care tag stated, "Do not machine wash. Do not hand wash. Do not dry clean." Fortunately, it was patterned in the four basic food group colors, so I was able to wear it until it was truly disgusting. Unfortunately, that didn't take long.

❀ **Souvenir shopping eats up precious vacation hours.** It's time that's better spent relaxing and recharging our batteries. Besides, do you, or does anyone back home, really need or want another mug, cap or T-shirt? I recently spent three rainy weeks studying castles and country homes at Oxford University in England. The last day there was a beauty, so I stretched out on a towel under a tree in the Merton College gardens, reading and soaking up rare rays of sunshine. I had the place practically to myself, since almost every other student was out frantically shopping for souvenirs, an exercise I gave up long ago. Instead, I've learned to bring home what travel guru Rick Steves calls "mental souvenirs"—recollections of a spectacular sunrise in the mountains, a day kayaking on a lake, a memorable meal in an outdoor café. My friends and family understand and are probably grateful, since they have more than enough trinkets and T-shirts.

> "Elegance does not consist in putting on a new dress."
>
> —Coco Chanel, fashion designer

Alternative Shopping

❀ **Swap rather than shop.** A group of eight similarly sized friends from a Los Angeles health club gets together every fall and spring to trade clothes that are "too nice to toss" but no longer fit or flatter. "Most of us go through fashion phases that either never worked in the first place or we out-grew," says swapper Debbi Lorenzo. "So my former peasant look might be just right for Kim who is about to be a stay-at-home mom. But it's our maternity clothes that see the most action." Other swap groups around the country are made up of coworkers, friends or extended family, and trade everything from household goods to baby equipment and kids' clothes.

> "Whether it's cups and saucers, clothing or property, think about why you're willing to swap your hard-earned money for it."
>
> —Dixie Carter, actress

❀ **Borrow, don't buy.** From ball gowns to yard tools, we can mooch or rent thousands of space-clogging, budget-busting occasional and one-time-use items, saving space, money and maintenance. I once lived in a close-knit neighborhood where a fifty-cup coffee maker was passed around so often, no one could remember who actually bought it.

❀ **Replace shopping with more gratifying pastimes.** Walking in the woods, reading a book, taking a class and volunteering take little equipment and are ultimately more satisfying than the never-ending pursuit of more stuff. As *New York Times* columnist William Safire pointed out, "Doing the outlet center does not stimulate the mind or recreate the body or satisfy the soul."

❀ **Spirituality increases contentment.** Whether it's regular prayer or meditation, a rich inner life satisfies from within so we need fewer trappings from without.

❀ **Observe a day of abstinence.** Adbusters, an international group of antimaterialistic activists bent on offering alternatives to our "shop-till-you-drop" lifestyle, hosts a Buy Nothing Day on the biggest consumer orgy of the year—the day after Thanksgiving. Instead of fighting the crowds to bag a bargain, give into that post-turkey tryptophan and make it a day of rest, renewal and relaxation.

> "There is one satisfying way to satisfy the way to live well and pay less: consume less."
>
> —Alexandra Stoddard, writer and interior designer

❀ **Delayed gratification can be rewarding.** When we take a Zen approach and wait patiently until we know exactly what we need, we often get exactly what we want. No more, no less.

> "There is one advantage to having nothing: It never needs repair."
>
> —Frank A. Clark, writer

❀ **Surround yourself with living things: people, pets and plants.** They're the best anecdote for a material-driven culture.

LIFE MATTERS:

The Stuff of Contentment

Who we are comes from the inside, not from the clothes we wear, the car we drive or the trappings we surround ourselves with. My father was one of the least materialistic people I've known. When he died, I was amazed at how few personal objects—a pipe stand, a scrapbook, a small, well-worn wardrobe—he left behind. Yet he was a happy man, working in his garden, supplying the neighborhood with the extra produce, driving a friend into the doctor every other week for years and taking pride in his children's and grandchildren's modest accomplishments. A simple man with simple tastes who knew the meaning of contentment.

The Shopping Habits of Mall Junkies

According to government figures and a 2003 survey by the International Council of Shopping Centers:

❀ New Yorkers spend the most money on clothes per household—$3,000 a year. San Franciscans spend $2,775, and Dallas-Fort Worth shoppers, $2,596.

"Objects can, at times, make us happy. But ultimately, do they give us what we really want?"

—Jane Hammerslough,
Dematerializing

❀ U.S. teens frequent a shopping mall on an average of 13 times within 3 months, spending 83.6 minutes and $46.80 per run.

❀ Americans between ages 35 and 44 visit a shopping mall 8.7 times within 3 months, spending 75.8 minutes and $81.70 per visit.

"Fashion stinks."
—Sentiment printed on
Billy Bob Thornton's
T-shirt at the 2004
Grammy Awards

❀ Shoppers between ages 45 and 54 average 9 visits in 3 months, spending 73.9 minutes and $84.40 each run.

❀ The longer one stays at a mall, the more he or she will spend: $134.20 on average if a trip lasts over 3 hours.

CHAPTER FIVE

Master Shopping

*"Shopping has a lot in common with sex:
Just about everybody does it. Some people brag about
how well they do it. Some keep it a secret. Most people
worry, at least a little, about whether they do it
right. And both sex and shopping provide ample
opportunities to make really foolish choices."*

—Thomas Hine,
I Want That: How We All Became Shoppers

Okay, so maybe we can't psyche ourselves into giving up shopping entirely. Things wear out, become outgrown and, worse, go out of fashion. Besides, shopping, especially clothes shopping, can be rewarding once it's mastered. Here are a few ideas for shopping so well that everything purchased will be well worn, well loved and never a source of clutter.

Preshopping Strategies

  ⎆ **Visualize finding exactly what you need at the price you want to pay.** Creative visualization works especially well for fashion

and furnishings, since clothing and household goods are so tangible. Not long ago, I needed a dress for an evening wedding. I knew almost everyone would be in basic black, so I wanted to stand out—but not too much. I thought long and hard about what I wanted till I could actually see myself moving in a claret-colored sheath. Shortly after, as I left a bookstore one night, I had a strong hunch I'd find exactly what I wanted in a nearby shop. And there it was, waiting for me—a simple, deep-red silk sheath. It is now the favorite thing in my wardrobe.

> "You can dress really well with very little money if you have taste—and perhaps courage."
>
> —Carmen, fashion model

⚬ **Evaluate your lifestyle.** Make a list of all the activities you do in a week, then check your closets to see if the clothes are compatible with your activities. When I made my list, I had a reality check. I have scads of dress-up clothes in my closet, yet I spend much of my time working alone in my home office, hiking, eating at casual restaurants and going to the movies. Since I'm pretty content with my life, I've finally figured out that I'm better off putting my shopping time and money into great-looking, comfortable sportswear than blowing the wad and the space on something I wear only once in a blue moon.

⚬ **Be ready for that blue moon.** Have one classic, perfectly tailored little black dress or its equivalent, along with the accompanying shoes, purse and jewelry, that you can rely on for special occasions.

Nothing fills a closet with mistakes faster than shopping for something elegant in an emergency.

✂ **Shop for your body type.** Are you tall and willowy? Small and muscular? Zaftig and sexy? Pay attention to what brings out the best in that unique body of yours, and go with the flow. Once I realized that darts and princess seams made me look like I actually have a waist, which I don't, it's made shopping a more focused and rewarding experience.

> "I base my fashion sense on what doesn't itch."
>
> —Gilda Radner, comedian

✂ **Know what rings your bell.** It could be a passion for Italian leather boots, a longing for vintage necklaces or a craving for cable-knit sweaters. Whatever it is, concentrate on it. It will not only define your personal style, it'll make you a more discriminating shopper.

✂ **Acknowledge what doesn't work.** A bracelet dangling off my wrist has always made me nervous. However, that didn't stop me from being seduced by a pretty one every so often. Unfortunately, my jewelry drawer has always had a more intimate relationship with these bangles than I have. Now that I see the error of my ways, I can move onto my true love: earrings.

✂ **Shop your closet.** "When I cleaned out my closet recently, I discovered where the holes were in my wardrobe," said professional organizer Irene Tobis. "I had plenty of jackets but not enough tops to wear under them." Once we identify our wardrobe's core pieces, it's easier to focus on what we need and ignore what we don't.

⚘ **Stick with your true colors.** Find your most flattering tones and shades by having your skin, hair and eye color professionally analyzed. According to Washington, D.C., image consultant Lynne Glassman, when we know which hues suit us best, we can simplify shopping by quickly dismissing clothes in unflattering colors while zeroing in on the most complementary. Another big perk is that once we find and shop our color range, everything in our closets blends beautifully. However, think of the recommended colors as a guide more than a commandment. Pegged as an "autumn," I was told my "basic black" was dark brown. Horse feathers! It is nearly impossible to find core pieces in dark brown; besides, I'm not crazy about the color. All the other colors chosen for me, however, have proved both flattering and good mixers.

⚘ **Focus on the details.** Rather than buying yet another outfit, plan to shop for an accessory that will pull existing clothes together and take up minimal storage space. A cashmere shawl that gracefully drapes over the shoulders, earrings in an eye-matching color or an important leather belt can make the difference between a so-so and a sensational outfit. "Accessories don't fall out of fashion as quickly as hem lengths and other whims of fashion," points out Lynne Glassman. "And you never hear anyone say, 'I just gained five pounds and can't fit into my new earrings.'"

"Clothes without accessories is like sex without orgasm."

—Robert Lee Morris, jewelry designer

- **Dress for the hunt.** When shopping, dress in comfortable shoes in the heel height you normally wear, nude colored underwear and a two-piece outfit so you don't need to drag an extra item into the dressing room or you aren't half-naked when trying on just a top or bottom. I find pants and a button-front sweater the perfect clothes-shopping uniform, since the top doesn't muss my makeup and hair as I slip it on and off.

- **Lighten the load.** I keep a small, fabric, hands-free shoulder bag in my trunk for serious shopping. I simply pop in my checkbook, a picture ID, a little cash, a comb and a lipstick. Hauling around anything more is draining. For security's sake, I discreetly lock the bigger purse in the trunk *before* I get to the store parking lot.

- **Get gorgeous.** Pay special attention to your makeup and hair to feel better about yourself under those ghastly fluorescent lights and intimidating three-way mirrors. A well-groomed customer also garners respect and thus attentiveness from the sales force. I recently shopped for a shower gift at a chichi kitchen shop. Dressed in an old warm-up, I had to practically prostrate myself in front of the cash register to get any help. A month before I had been there dressed to the nines with my best purse—a clerk-impressing prop—on my way to a party. The help couldn't have been more helpful.

- **Be loyal.** There's a lot to be said for sticking with one or two stores that fit your style and budget, especially since it's easier to keep track of the store's layout, merchandise and personnel.

My friend Diane always shops at a department store known for its superb service, though its sales are few and far between. "Sure, there might be a better deal down the street, but I know I can waste precious time and energy hunting for it," she explained. "I simply don't have that time."

⚐ **Be a label connoisseur.** Make note of labels that flatter your body shape, and seek them out. A manufacturer that offers a good cut for particular figure features can be almost as good as having a personal dressmaker.

⚐ **Be a realist.** Buy clothing that fits your current body, not a past or a hoped-for future size.

> "I wear what makes me feel good, not something a designer says is current."
> —Halle Berry

⚐ **Get personal.** If your favorite store has a personal shopper on staff, consider booking an appointment. The service is free, and because a personal shopper is familiar with everything in the store, she or he can zoom in on exactly what you need at a price you can afford, whether it's as simple as a special occasion top or as daunting as a Christmas list. A personal shopper can also tell you when a desired item is likely to go on sale and hold it for you. "Establishing a relationship with a personal shopper is a smart move on anyone's part," maintains Andrea Silber, a manager at an upscale department store. "Once one knows your style, your budget and your favorite colors, he or she can save you hours of unnecessary hunting."

Freelance writer Lynne Friedman agrees. Ten years ago, when she was asked to run the news briefings at the annual, weeklong meeting of the American Association for the Advancement of Science, she asked a personal shopper to update three still serviceable suits she planned to pack for the event. "My budget was tight, but I needed to look polished and camera-ready since I was in charge of the news briefings," said Friedman. "A Nordstrom personal shopper was able to punch things up with a few blouses, a couple of belts, some costume jewelry and new shoes. She also suggested I shorten the skirts. So for $400, I got eleven outfits and a whole new look. It was so much more cost and time effective than if I did it myself."

"Personal shoppers may be the best kept secret in retail," affirms Steve Boorstein, author of *The Ultimate Guide to Shopping & Caring for Clothing*. "They do the legwork for you, select accessories for the clothes, offer fashion advice, provide a tailor and a great dressing room. In the end, they'll save you time, money and frustration so you can channel your energies elsewhere."

> "Fashion is a form of ugliness so intolerable that we have to alter it every six months."
>
> —Oscar Wilde, writer

⚖ **Call before you search.** This strategy works best for specific items, like a leather jacket or suede gloves. Once the item has been located, ask the clerk to tag it with your name and hold it at the cash register for you. Make sure to get the clerk's name as well, so he or she will take responsibility for the job.

Go Forth and Gather

❀ **Shop alone.** It's natural for most people to be drawn to colors and styles that look best on *them,* not you, and a partner can be the worst. My husband, for instance, will talk me into buying almost anything I try on just to get me out of the store and end his misery.

❀ **Be timely.** For the widest and freshest selection, shop just after Independence Day for fall and winter clothes, just after Christmas for spring attire and just after Easter for summer things.

> "I'd rather hang by my ovaries than try on pants in front of my mother."
> —Patricia Volk, writer

❀ **Only buy what you absolutely love.** "It should look great in the store and great 72 hours after you bought it," said Steve Boorstein. "If you want a truly smart wardrobe, stop buying 'maybes.'" Clothes are like men—if you settle for the mediocre, you may not be able to have the marvelous when it shows up.

❀ **Stock up.** When you find a great basic, buy multiples. I don't know how many times I've found what I considered the perfect bra, only to find it discontinued when I went back to replace it. Just after I found my last good one, I called the lingerie department and ordered four. As a bonus, the clerk suggested I wait a week till it went on a two-for-one sale, so I got them at half price. A good bra is like having good bone structure, everything drapes better over it.

❀ **Buy quality.** "You'll forget the price tag fast enough, but that blazer will be with you for years," maintains Kim Johnson Gross and Jeff Stone in *Chic Simple: Work Clothes.*

❀ **Invest in pieces worn close to the face.** With all respect to big breasts and a perky butt, it's human nature to focus the eye on the face more than on any other part of the body. Frame it with flattering color and nice detailing.

❀ **Recognize fly-by-night fashion.** Fads are fun, but it's not so smart to blow the wad on something that will look dated in a season. Better to have a fling with lime green eye shadow than with a lime green winter coat, unless, of course, lime green is your signature color.

"I really hate being too hip. It makes me feel like a dog in pajamas."

—Jewel

❀ **Educate yourself.** Before buying something mechanical, whether it's a car, a major appliance or a TV, call an independent repair service to see which brands and models are most trouble free. The fewer the glitches, the longer an item will last.

❀ **Know what's important.** "Always buy a good bed and a good pair of shoes. If you're not in one, you're in the other," advises British talk-show host Gloria Hunniford.

Buyer Beware

⚷ **Be cautious with sales.** Face it, with the exception of a few basics, like the previously mentioned bras, things usually go on sale because they were either overpriced the first time around or, worse, shipped in just for the sale. A friend of mine worked in the men's department of a high-end, nationally respected department store. He divulged that the store brought in truckloads of inferior merchandise specifically for their famous twice-yearly sales. I tested his claim by cruising the store the afternoon before one big event. Notices were posted announcing an early closing that evening so employees could discount merchandise. The next day, I found little that I recognized from my reconnaissance mission. Some of it was nice, some of it was cheap, but little of it was on the floor the day before. Some sales are genuine, but unless we stick to exactly what we need, marked-down merchandise can be a major source of clutter. Even when sales are for real, it's too easy to buy something just because it's cheap, not because we love it or need it. As model and beauty writer Diane Irons says, "It's only a good buy if you would pay full price for it."

> "Bargain: something you can't use at a price you can't resist."
> —Franklin P. Jones, writer

- ✂ **Never buy an item of clothing without trying it on and thoroughly examining it first.** "Otherwise," maintains professional organizer Irene Tobis, "we lock ourselves into an endless cycle of buying and returning, driving to and from the mall."

- ✂ **Never buy anything that doesn't go with at least three items of clothing you already own.** That coral print pencil skirt might be pretty, but you'll eat up precious time and energy looking for compatible mates.

- ✂ **Shop only where returns are hassle free.** Even with the best-laid plans, mistakes happen. The new shoes pinch, the boucle pants bag at the knees, the angora sweater puffs us up like a cumulus cloud. Besides, we all have a change of heart occasionally, so we shouldn't have to pay the price of long lines, short grace periods and sour sales clerks. National chains like Nordstrom and Rite Aid take a generous stance on returns, but it pays to check out a store's policy *before* you buy.

"When you are in love with someone, you want to be near him all the time, except when you are out buying things and charging them to him."

—Miss Piggy

☙ **Be careful with credit.** Either we have the money for purchases or we don't, and paying 18 percent interest can sink us into debt faster than stones in our swimsuits. Paying the bill within the month is always an option, but it just adds to the mound of paperwork. Besides, saving for a particular item helps us evaluate its importance and makes the purchase ultimately more satisfying.

The Ten Commandments of Clutter-Free Shopping

"Happiness is the best look."

—Isaac Mizrahi, fashion designer

Clutter is all the stuff that clogs our lives, complicates cleaning, and we are better off without it. Trouble is, it's also the stuff we have most of. Here are tried and true ways to nip clutter's accumulation in the bud.

1. **Avoid braking for garage sales, swap meets, flea markets and dumps.** They are the genesis of junk as well as weekend wasters.

2. **Limit your shopping time.** The more time we spend in a store, claims professional organizer Irene Tobis, the more unnecessary items we buy. I was just on my way to the parking lot after buying a baby gift when my husband called to warn me of a major accident on the freeway. "Wait it out till after rush hour," he advised. I did as suggested and, after two hours of aimless browsing, ended up hauling home three books I've yet to read, a vase that's never held flowers and a fifth pair of black pants.

3. **Hold out for quality furnishings.** When my husband and I could no longer stand living with painters and plumbers during our remodel, we rented a furnished apartment for a month. The decor was pretty enough, but like a Hollywood set, it was only for show. The chairs were stiff, the sofa sagged and the table wobbled. When quality is compromised, comfort and durability are lost, and we end up shopping and replacing things more than we should.

4. **Buy one exquisite thing rather than two or three "good-enoughs."** Buying so-so stuff is like eating so-so food. Both make us feel so-so, so we end up consuming more than we need. Yet we're seldom satisfied.

5. **Never buy clothes, dishes or linens that scream holiday.** The Santa skirt, the jack-o-lantern platter, the shamrock tablecloth. Better to wear and use the color of the day than a motif that's dated the day after.

6. **Don't be a fashion victim.** A belt or a hat in the style of the moment is one thing, but buying into the season's whole look is a lousy investment. Stick to the classics: a perfectly fitted jacket in a flattering color and quality fabric, nicely cut pants, a good purse, beautifully designed and comfortable shoes. Update with the fun stuff, but be timely not trendy.

7. **Stick to a list.** Number it in order of importance, and focus on the most important item. A list keeps us from being overwhelmed by a multitude of choices in the marketplace. Besides, impulse buying is a lot like impulse eating—we pay the price for excess in the end.

8. **Avoid bonus-with-purchase offers.** You know the deal. You buy the mascara, but for just $20 more, you can have a train case filled with three shades of blush, foundation and a lipstick. The trouble is, every item in stock is just under $20, so you'll need to buy at least two of something. Who needs three shades of blush, foundation that doesn't match and a tube of neon-orange lipstick anyway? And who needs a carry-on that won't hold half of what we need on a trip?

> "When women are depressed, they eat or go shopping. Men invade another country. It's a whole different way of thinking."
>
> —Elayne Boosler, comedian

9. **Ask for free samples of cosmetics and toiletries you'd like to try.** Most department stores, skin-care salons and dermatologist's offices have them. Tiny samples not only allow us to test before we invest, they also save money and drawer

and counter space. They also tuck neatly into a handbag or suitcase.

10. **Give something nice away when you come home with something new.** It's good clutter control and great karma.

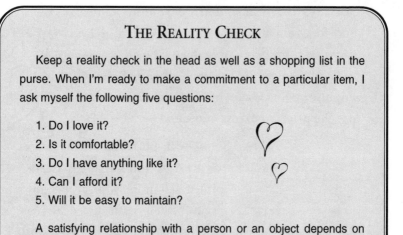

THE REALITY CHECK

Keep a reality check in the head as well as a shopping list in the purse. When I'm ready to make a commitment to a particular item, I ask myself the following five questions:

1. Do I love it?
2. Is it comfortable?
3. Do I have anything like it?
4. Can I afford it?
5. Will it be easy to maintain?

A satisfying relationship with a person or an object depends on more than love at first sight.

LIFE MATTERS:

Be Psy-Chic

Are you drawn to certain looks because you crave a different lifestyle? Does that flippy fuchsia skirt signify a stuffed urge to tango? Does that black leather jacket mean you're finally ready for that Harley? Does a craving for silk tap pants and a lace bustier tell you its time to take a lover?

The clothes we find so impractical yet so seductive can tell us a lot about our hidden hopes and dreams. My former client Diane is a freelance writer who lives in warm-ups and jeans, yet when she shops, she's drawn to long skirts and elegant tops—things that have long languished in her closet. She finally figured a way to merge her wardrobe wants with her lifestyle: She became a fund-raising volunteer for the San Diego Opera, where she not only sashays about in her silks and slingbacks, but she's also met the man of her dreams. Maybe it *is* time to lay off the sensible basics we've always bought and focus on something that will make life juicier.

CHAPTER SIX

The Closet-rophobia Cure

*"Everything is coming out of the closet
these days, except clutter."*

—Don Aslett, *Clutter Free*

I've lived with a claustrophobic closet most of my life. At times it was so crammed, I'd hang things in the bathroom just so I wouldn't have to face the stacks of shoes, the squished shirts and the collapsing piles of sweaters. But every so often, particularly when I'd purge the surplus and rotate the seasonal, tidiness reigned.

> "The amount of time it takes for you to leave the house in the morning is directly proportional to the number of shoes in your closet."
>
> —Leigh Anne Jasheway, writer

The newly organized closet would initially buoy me, but my lack of space and messy ways would eventually do me in. My husband, Larry, on the other hand, didn't have this problem, since he has the habit of hanging up his things daily and updating his wardrobe on the average of every other leap year. A good thing, since I appropriated much of his closet long ago.

One day, shortly after our youngest left for college, we put the house on the market. It's a nice house, so we expected a quick sale. It didn't happen. Buyers saw the kitchen as tiny and the master bedroom closet as ridiculously cramped. I saw the kitchen as cozy. As for the closet, I'd gotten as used to my clothes getting stuffed in this cubicle as I'd gotten used to my body getting stuffed on an airplane. But prospective buyers seemed to want their clothes hanging in first class or not at all.

Wanting to get a first-class price for the house, we checked with a contractor friend about the feasibility of upgrading both areas. "Piece of cake," he said.

"You'll likely get your money back," confirmed the Realtor, since property values in our neck of the woods had recently skyrocketed. So as well as jazzing up the kitchen, we expanded and redesigned the closet. It's now a modest walk-in closet, divided into his-and-hers halves by a built-in chest of drawers and lighted and ventilated by a small north window. We felt so good about the transformation, we decided to take the house off the market and enjoy our newly liberated wardrobes.

> "If you want to forget all your troubles, wear shoes that are too tight."
> —Mildred Watts, writer

Since it's one of the first things I see in the morning and the last thing I see at night, I believe our new closet affects both my waking and my sleeping hours. If the closet is a mess, I not only look a mess, I feel a mess. But it's now so easy to keep things in shape—my shoes seldom fling themselves into dusty heaps and my grungy sweats hardly ever rub against my delicate silks.

I figure if I can exert such control over my clothes, maybe I can control more important areas of my life. Today the closet, tomorrow the world.

The Seven Habits of Highly Effective Closets

In the process of upgrading my own and my clients' closets, I've learned there's much that can be improved without resorting to expensive and traumatic surgery. I've also discovered that every closet, big or small, benefits from the following:

1. **Easy access.** Sliding doors are not only heavy, they obscure part of the wardrobe all the time. Better to have standard full-swing or bifold doors. This way, you can consider all clothing options at a glance. Draperies are also a workable option, since they take less space and give a room visual softness.

2. **Versatility.** Shelves, hanging rods and drawer systems are better flexible than fixed, since closet needs change with wardrobe needs, and wardrobe needs change with the times. Who knows? With the emphasis on retro fashion, bustles and petticoats could soon be taking over our closets.

3. **Effective lighting.** I blame the black hole of my old closet for the time I wore one black shoe and one navy shoe to a speaking engagement. Luckily, the podium mostly hid me. I've since discovered I could have easily remedied the situation with a self-sticking, battery-operated "touch" light. With the new closet, we opted for incandescent lighting (the same type of bulb used in conventional table lamps), since it has a more natural cast than fluorescent lighting and is safer than halogen

bulbs. (Halogen bulbs get hot enough to torch anything near them.)

4. **Visible storage.** In addition to being able to see hanging clothes, it's good to be able to spot folded stuff without having to lift box lids and rummage through drawers. I find that clear plastic storage boxes, wire rollout bins and portable, rod-hung canvas shelves make for quick and rumple-free identification.

5. **Reflectiveness.** White, high-gloss paint is a good choice for closet walls, since the color best reflects light, and the slick finish deflects dust. We made the mistake of covering our closet walls with cedar boards, which are nice for moth control and fragrance but way too dark. We later discovered that cedar must be sanded at least once a year to release its moth-repellent scent. Who wants to evacuate their entire wardrobe for that?

6. **Primp potential.** A big, well-lit, full-length mirror in the closet saves steps to another room to check falling hems and peek-a-boo labels. A mirror also reflects light and makes the closet seem larger. If you can't hang a mirror in your closet or on its door, hang one close by. Place a chair near it as well to see how clothes behave when you are seated.

7. **Breathing room.** It's important to be highly selective about adequate spacing behind closed doors—a tightly packed closet leads to wrinkles, indecisiveness and, ultimately, chaos. Each piece of hung clothing should get within no closer than a light kiss of each other.

Clothing and the Quality of Life

Navigating through great gobs of clothes when all we need is our favorite T-shirt is like navigating through great gobs of goods at a mega-mart when all we need is a quart of milk. It's so much easier to get dressed when our closets hold only the crème de la crème of clothes.

Television's Deborah Norville can vouch for that: "The fewer choices you have, the less time you spend making decisions," she said in a *Family Circle* magazine interview. "In recent years, as my family has grown bigger and my life has become more complicated, I have made a conscious decision to limit the new that comes in," she said. "I stick to the basics and add something trendy or colorful only on occasion."

Secrets of a Solid Wardrobe Core

❀ Pare down to only the clothes you love. Life is too short for so-so clothes.

❀ Know and narrow your look. You may like East Coast preppy and West Coast flash, but you're probably more one than the other. Some of the most chichi people on the planet—women like Audrey Hepburn, Katharine Hepburn, Coco Chanel and Jackie Kennedy— knew what look suited them best and stuck with it. "You have to know what looks good on you," said actress Minnie Driver.

> "Notice how you feel surrounded by things you love, people you love, and clothes you love wearing."
>
> —Susan Reeve,
> *Choose Peace & Happiness*

"And not 'Well, that looked good on Cindy Crawford. I'll wear that.'"

❀ Plan a wardrobe around a few complementary core neutrals that work well together. Camel, cream, gray and black, for instance, are classic colors that never look dated, are interchangeable and mix well with seasonal colors. Department store manager Andrea Silber says she always advises her new salesclerks to buy a fine-quality, classic black suit. "With less-expensive trendy tops, a lacy camisole and maybe a twin set, you can wear that same suit three times a week," she said. The idea is to have a minimum of pieces that you can wear in a maximum of combinations.

"If you don't see the same people every day, all you need in your closet are two great outfits."

—Emily Cho, *Instant Style*

❀ When possible, buy the matching or coordinating top or bottom for mixing and matching. I once bought two matching pant and sweater sets—one in gray and one in camel—that turned out to be the most versatile combo in my closet.

❀ Focus on the dark. "Darker colors," points out Elaine St. James in *Living the Simple Life*, "are easier to work with from season to season and lend an aura of quality and professionalism to your total look." Dark colors also demand less cleaning.

❀ Get more out of basics by buying them in year-round fabrics. A lightweight wool jacket, fine-gauge silk or cotton sweaters, lined microfiber trousers and long-sleeved cotton T-shirts are classic season-spanners. For the past four summers, when I've packed for nearly a month in England, where temperatures swing from the tropical to the arctic, these pieces have seen me through.

✿ Find a fine-quality handbag that goes with almost everything so you seldom have to switch.

✿ Add pizazz to basics with fun jewelry, bright scarves and textured belts. A small but select wardrobe is like a well-decorated room: versatile, interesting and classic.

Double Your Closet Space

Even with the most carefully planned wardrobe, finding space for it can be challenging for the clotheshorses many of us are. One of the easiest ways to create it is the seasonal switch—the spring and fall ritual when sundresses or sweaters come out of the attic or out from under the bed and trade places. It can be a big undertaking, but reacquainting yourself with cherished clothes you haven't seen for six months is almost like unwrapping presents on Christmas.

I usually break down the process into several 15- to 30-minute sessions in one week, sometimes listening to a library book on tape as I make the transfer. Other times, I've used it as a kind of quiet meditation, assessing each item on its condition, fit, fashion status and whether I wore it last season. Those things that don't make the cut are out the door within the week.

> "One of the principles of organization is to limit your choices."
> —Sandra Felton, writer

DISCOVER THE PERFECT COLOR SCHEME

Closets have long been the stashing spots for the family jewels and skeletons. With an observant eye, you may find that the perfect decorating scheme is hidden there as well.

One of my first interior design clients was a woman who was bored with her "safe" white walls, beige carpeting and earth-tone furnishings, but she was at a loss as to how to spice them up without spending a fortune. I checked out her closet and discovered her wardrobe was a Monet study in soft blues, greens and lavender, colors that turned out to be the perfect palette for her walls, slipcovers, pillows, towels and other easily changed goods throughout her home.

With her china blue eyes, fair skin and platinum hair, she ended up "wearing" her surroundings beautifully.

On the other end of the spectrum, fashion designer Eileen Fisher has every room in her New York home painted in a signature palette of bone or stone. She even has one room matched to a raincoat in her current clothing line.

The Top Ten Closet Cloggers

Every closet has its clingers and cloggers—those items that hog closet space yet serve no useful purpose to anyone. The following are the top ten offenders:

1. **Wire hangers.** They tangle, they snag, they rust, they contort clothes. Since most of us are fighting nature's paunches and puckers, who needs manufactured ones? Better to buy a supply of plastic, wood and padded hangers. Padded hangers are perfect for delicate silks and hangable knits. Plastic skirt hangers are good for pants, too. Plastic tubular models are good

all-around workhorses. Wood hangers, especially fragrant, bug-busting cedar models, are good for heavy items like coats and jackets. I like the plump, curved ones that retain the shape of the garment and maintain a bit of breathing space between clothes.

2. **Frayed and grayed underwear.** Mom was right. We *could* end up in the emergency room. The embarrassment may be worse than the pain, especially when that cute paramedic checks for vital signs.

3. **Ratty robes and sleepwear.** It's hard enough to get up in the morning without facing what looks like an *Extreme Makeover* candidate in the mirror.

4. **Too many "dirty work" outfits.** One hair-coloring outfit and one grubby gardening getup are more than enough for any wardrobe.

5. **Clothes for all we *meant* to do but never got around to doing.** Taking up tennis, throwing a Saint Patrick's Day party, becoming a rock star. It's good to have *dreams* for the future, but an effective closet holds only *clothes* for the present.

6. **Stretched swimsuits.** With faith and discipline, the body can spring back into its former shape, but that baggy spandex never will.

7. **Skinny clothes.** "Keeping those jeans that don't fit you anymore as inspiration to diet?" asks Carson Kressley from *Queer Eye for the Straight Guy.* "Cute. But Weight Watchers is more effective."

8. **Shoes too shot to repair.** Prada or Payless, nothing ruins an outfit like a shabby pair of footwear.

9. **Stockings with runs and snags.** Sure we can do the old cut-the-leg-off-wear-two-pair trick, but do we really want to be strangled by *multiple* waistbands?

10. **Abandoned socks.** Face it. Socks too can find a better life. That cute little anklet was probably too good for him anyway.

Four Top-Drawer Tactics

1. Fill drawers in get-dressed order. Underwear in the top drawer, socks and stockings in the middle and pajamas in the bottom.

2. Use snap-in drawer dividers or lidless shoe boxes to sort and store items so they're easy to see, retrieve and keep tidy.

3. Line drawers with scented paper. It not only protects against wood snags, it adds a subtle mood-lifting fragrance to clothing and closet. Liner lost its scent? Remove the clothes from the drawer. Spray the paper with your best cologne. Let dry. Add clothes.

4. Be careful with potpourri. Direct contact between certain spices and fabrics can leave its mark.

Get the Hang of It

☙ Move clothes that you wear most often to where they're easiest to see and reach. I hang my favorite pants near the front of the closet and the tops that go with them on the rod just above.

⚶ Want to save scads of time in the morning? Nail a hefty hook into the back of the closet door to hang the next day's outfit, including underwear and accessories.

⚶ Some clothes are incompatible rod-mates. Molters, like white angora, should never hang out with magnets, like black velvet.

⚶ Keep empty hangers accessible by hanging them at the end of a specified rod.

Shelving Smarts

⚘ Shallow (12" deep) shelves are best in closets. We're apt to overload and lose items on deeper ones.

⚘ Consider shelf dividers to keep sweater and sweatshirt towers from toppling into each other. Rubbermaid makes a set for under $10 that neatly divides three stacks of sweaters into boutique order.

> "I realize there are certain hardships that only females must endure, such as childbirth, waiting lines for public restroom stalls and a crippling psychotic obsession with shoe color."
>
> —Dave Barry, humorist

⚘ Don't stack wool sweaters more than three high. Wool, like most natural fabrics, stays fresh and perky when it has breathing room.

⚘ Round up space invaders like purses, and wayward items like gloves, in rectangular baskets. Mufflers and knit hats also stay handy when corralled in their own baskets.

⚘ Shelve shoes with the toes facing inward so you can consider at a glance the all-crucial heel height.

Low-Tech Tools for Keeping Order

There are some pretty sophisticated and pricey gadgets out there for keeping closets in apple pie order. But like much in life, simple is often superior. Here are some of the best tidiers:

- **Wall hooks.** In addition to segregating the next day's or evening's outfit, they're good for hanging hats, purses, pajamas and scarves. They're also nice for those nights when some of us (we know who we are) are just too pooped to use a real hanger. Buy fat hooks, which are less apt to leave their mark on fabric.

- **Shopping bags.** Keep one in the corner of the closet for collecting castoffs. Once it's full, toss it into the car trunk and ferry it to your favorite charity.

- **Zippered mesh laundry bags.** Hang one for dark delicates and another for lights on a hook or a hanger. When full, simply toss it in the gentle cycle.

- **Rod dividers.** These are similar to the plastic ones department stores use to separate clothing sizes. I make mine by tracing a dozen saucer-sized circles on poster board. I then trace a rod-sized jar lid in the middle of each circle, cut a slit to it, and then cut out the hole and the full circle. I slip the dividers over the closet rod between items I want to separate—short-sleeve T-shirts from long-sleeve ones, dress pants from jeans and khakis, turtlenecks from polo shirts, and so on. I find they're a good reminder to put things back where they belong. And I need all the reminders I can get.

- **Rubber bands.** Wrap them around the ends of plastic hangers to keep slippery straps from slipping off.

☙ **A decent-sized wastebasket.** Essential for deep-sixing pocket trash, wire hangers and hopeless underwear. It's surprising how many closets lack such a necessity.

> "It is a pleasure to wake up in the morning and know exactly where everything is."
>
> —Anthony Vidergauz, president of California Closets

Uncommon Storage Alternatives

Free up the bedroom closet and increase convenience with the following off-site possibilities.

❀ Store a gorgeous gown in the hallway closet to free up the bedroom closet and to dazzle guests as you hang their coats.

❀ Drape shawls over the arms of easy chairs and sofas for curl-up warmth. I have a lush, politically incorrect red fox jacket that was given to me long ago. I never wear it; but rather than letting it hog the closet or languish in the attic, I've tucked the arms under so it drapes over a sofa arm like a blanket. It makes for mighty fine cuddling on a cold night.

❀ Stash space-hogging, dirt-depositing athletic shoes and snow boots on a rack in the garage or utility room so they're handy to the outdoors and won't track muck through the house. I store our grubby footwear in an old bookcase in the garage. I know a serious gardener who keeps hers under a garden bench in her utility room—a comfortable spot to switch from boots to bedroom slippers.

❀ Keep a T-shirt, shorts, warm-up gear and a pair of athletic shoes in the trunk of the car for a spontaneous workout and to free up closet space. I stash a hat and sunblock there as well, so when I have thirty minutes or more between errands, I can change shoes, wriggle into a T-shirt and hit the streets.

❀ Old suitcases make dandy seasonal storage containers, provided they're not too big and can be easily retrieved from wherever they're stored.

❀ Hang chains from pegs on the closet wall or door back. They'll stay tangle-free and easy to reach, and they make a pretty display.

❀ Enjoy the psychological benefits of a streamlined closet. Losing surplus clothes is like losing surplus weight. We feel lighter, freer and better about ourselves.

> "I find a sense of calm when I open the door (to my closet) and find everything in order."
>
> —Janet Sobesky,
> *Woman's Day* magazine

CLEAR THE CLOSET, CLEAR THE MIND

Straightening a closet, or even just a closet shelf, has been known to help more than a few people work through some of life's bigger messes. When Marie Costello's father was hospitalized with depression, she was eight months pregnant with her second child and thus unable to make the long trek from San Francisco to Seattle.

"I put all my energies and frustrations into my closet, tossing things out and straightening the keepers, just like I wanted to toss out illness and straighten out my father's problems," she said. "For someone who's not that organized, I found the whole process strangely soothing and nurturing."

DESIGN FOR LIVING

Double Your Hanging Space

When my daughter Kelley moved into her first apartment, a good portion of her wardrobe sat in boxes for months, since her standard eight-foot-wide, eight-foot high, two-foot deep, one-pole closet could only accommodate about ninety-two items of clothing. Eventually, her fairy godmother (aka Mom) came to the rescue and elevated the pole to about eighty inches from the floor and installed a second pole about forty inches beneath it. The new space not only doubled her hanging capacity, it also organized it into pants and skirts on the bottom rod and tops on the top.

Luckily, she didn't need long hanging space for dresses and coats. If you do need this space, it can be easily created by installing a bolt-in closet divider (found in home improvement stores).

LIFE MATTERS:

Control Your Closet,
Change Your Life

"Imagine how good life can be with an ordered, pared down, highly selective closet," suggests author and professional organizer Julie Morgenstern, who believes in focusing on the payoff, not the problem.

Those payoffs could include on-time performance, since we can now find what we need when we need it; boosted confidence, since we now look polished; more energy, since we no longer wear ourselves out from rummaging through stacks of sweaters and heaps of shoes; and a new sense of serenity, since a well-groomed closet is such a soothing site on a rushed day.

Who knows where it all could lead? When order conquers chaos, new worlds emerge.

Part II

Comfort is more than a soft throw on a cold night.
It's a convenient place to stash stuff,
an easy way to outwit dirt, and a quiet,
softly lit space to escape to when all hell is
breaking loose. Investing in a little comfort
pays big dividends in contentment.

Invest in Comfort

CHAPTER SEVEN

Storing Earthly Goods

*"Do not lay up for yourselves treasures
on earth where moth and rust consume and
where thieves break in and steal."*

—Matthew 6:21

When Zoë, Jack and their baby, Chloe, moved from their tiny condo in Chicago to a relatively spacious bungalow in nearby Evanston, they thought they had finally found room for everything they owned and then some.

It didn't take long to reach "then some." The attic quickly filled with seasonal gear and Zoë's collection of "almost antique" furnishings she plans to refurbish and sell on eBay. The basement is stuffed with baby equipment, boxes of magazines, textbooks, sports trophies and craft projects in various stages of progression. And now that the garage has reached critical mass, the SUV sits in the driveway.

> "Only in America do we park costly cars in the driveway and park worthless junk in the garage."
>
> —Unknown

"We're thinking about renting a self-storage unit in town just to get the car in the garage for the winter," said Zoë. "I hate to pay for space when we already seem to have tons of it, but we have so much stashed around here, we can't always find what we need. Besides, does anyone ever have enough space?"

> "You can't have everything. Where would you put it?"
>
> —Ann Fox Chodakowski and Susan Fox Wood, *Living on a Shoestring*

Rarely. We want space in our relationships, jobs and our homes—especially in their stashing places—but there's seldom enough.

Yet there are ways to find it and make it work for everything that's worthy of being kept. First, we have to get a grip on the meat of the matter.

Three Storage Truths

1. **Usage is more important than storage.** Baby Chloe is already too big for outfits she never wore because they just seemed too good to be spit up on, and Zoë and Jack haven't yet used the gift-quality towels and bedding eating up closet space—practices many of us subscribe to. We need to ask ourselves what we're saving the good stuff for anyway. A visit from royalty? A little lunch for the president? Why can't we mortals enjoy "Sunday best" daily?

2. **All that's held should be loved.** The ugly clock Grandpa bequeathed isn't going to look any better in another year, and it's doubtful that the puce and olive rug moldering in Zoë and Jack's garage will ever grow on them. I had plans of quality cuddling when I bought a rocking chair just before my second daughter Lisa was born. But the chair was so back-breakingly

uncomfortable, I'd move to the recliner instead. Did I get rid of this instrument of torture? Only after two moves, twenty years of storage and a hold-the-nose scraping of mouse droppings.

3. **Birds of a feather are best flocked together.** From clothing to canned soup, possessions are easier to access when they're stored as a group in one spot. Zoë stored some seasonal clothes in a hall closet, others in a trunk at the end of the bed and the rest in the attic. "I could never remember what was where when a winter heat wave or a summer cool spell hit till I got a couple of rolling garment racks and hung every-thing in the attic," she said. "They've made a huge difference."

> "Order is the shape upon which beauty depends."
> —Pearl S. Buck, writer

The Holy Trinity of Storage

Once we recognize the differences among the three types of stor-age—working, hibernating and comatose—it's easier to find what we need when we need it. The following are simple strategies for managing all three:

I. Working Storage

Working storage encompasses currently worn clothing, active papers and all the equipment we use on a day-to-day basis. Adopt the following strategies for freer flowing days:

- Stash it where you use it. Keep extra blankets in a chest at the foot of the bed, position the coffeemaker near the water dis-penser and shelve frequently referenced books at eye level.

"Good storage is all about identifying what's important and having it at your fingertips so you can have the life that you want," maintains *Organizing from the Inside Out* author Julie Morgenstern.

- **Clear the decks.** Countertops, tabletops and desktops are for working, not storing. It's best to install whatever you can *around* high-use surfaces to keep them clear of clutter: spatulas and slotted spoons in a drawer below the cook-top, a wall-hung lamp above a desk, tools on a shelf beside a worktable. I kept my toiletries out on the bathroom counter for years simply because they seemed more convenient there. But once I sorted them in small bins and stashed them in drawers and cabinets, not only did I find that the counter was easier to clean and keep clean, but I also finally had the space to blow dry my hair without knocking over a battalion of bottles and jars.

- **Manage mobile matter.** I've set up a launching pad by the back door where I keep a wide, shallow basket for library books to be returned, mail to be mailed, as well as water and snacks for the car. Maria McKay, a mother of four, has a deep cabinet by the door to the garage with a shelf labeled for each member of the family. "We try to stack everything that's going out in the morning the night before," she explained. "It's a good way for outgoing items to be gone but not forgotten."

- **Dump the doubles.** Multiple sets of dishes, glassware and cookware eat up precious storage space. I have a friend who lugged around a 200-piece gold-banded heirloom china service from state to state for twelve years. She displayed it in a huge china cabinet, but never actually *used* it, since (1) it was too baroque for her streamlined tastes, (2) it couldn't be machine washed and (3) she wanted to give it to one of her daughters on her marriage. When wedding bells rang, first one daughter, then the other turned down the offer. "Too fussy" was the consensus. After twenty-five years, three moves and a hogging of prime cabinet space, the set is now gathering dust in a consignment shop.

> "I have a place for everything; where it lands."
> —Jennifer Stein, writer

AN OPEN-AND-SHUT CASE

Unless you're as persnickety as Felix Unger of *The Odd Couple* or as obsessive as Bree Van De Kamp of *Desperate Housewives,* open shelving, especially in high-use areas like the kitchen, bathroom and garage, tends to get messy. Better to hide the potentially unruly behind closed doors or curtains than to let it all hang out.

II. Hibernating Storage

Hibernating storage includes seasonal gear, holiday decorations and other things that alternate between deep sleep and high activity.

- ❀ Keep seasonal sports equipment, outdoor furnishings and all but clothing and upholstery fabric dust- and rust-free in super-size plastic bags. Fabric is best stored in fabric bags, since plastic can yellow it.

❧ Find the best buys on storage containers in August and September
for the new school year and
December and January for those
"gotta get organized" New Year's
resolutions.

> "There should be a
> certain amount of order
> because we cannot really
> rest in a disorderly place."
>
> —Elsie de Wolfe,
> early twentieth-century
> interior designer

❧ Use transparent bags, boxes and
bins for a quick surveillance of all
that's stashed without having to lift a lid or squint at a label.

❧ Choose rectangular containers over round ones, since they're
more space efficient on shelves.

❧ Stash all that's stackable on shelves or pallets so floors are easier
to sweep and swab. Off-the-floor items are also less apt to be
affected by seeping water, creeping mold and hungry varmints.

❧ Make stacking easy by using the same size containers. Pile
them no more than three or four high, both for safety and
easy retrieval.

❧ Create a storage loft in the garage or attic by laying 4' x 8' plywood sheets across the ceiling beams for lightweight seasonal
stuff. No beams? Consider a see-through storage unit of vinyl-
coated steel grids that hangs 18" to 24" from the ceiling. Check
out the latter at a home center or call Hyloft: 888-220-8493.

❧ Take the department store approach to organizing goods by
separating big storage areas, like the attic, garage and basement, into distinct departments—auto supplies, sports gear,
holiday decorations, women's wear, linens and so on. Keep
their borders defined but flexible by outlining the floors or
walls between them with chalk.

❀ Keep synthetic Christmas wreaths and garlands dust-free by wrapping them in plastic dry cleaner bags and hanging them from hooks nailed into attic or garage rafters. Better yet, free storage space by pruning or buying fresh ever-greens, then mulching the garden with them after the holidays.

"The stuff stays here. I'm renting a storage space so I can go sit in a nice empty room."

—*Cathy*, a comic strip by Cathy Guisewite

FOUR FABRIC-STORING SMARTS

1. Clean *all* off-season fabrics before storing. It takes only one soiled sweater to lure pests into a stack of clean ones. Hidden body oils and food dribbles not only turn into stains in time, they also invite pests to pull up a sleeve and dine.

2. Never starch any fabric before packing it away. Starch is a tasty treat to all kinds of critters.

3. Plastic can yellow and even rot heirloom linens. Better to wrap fabrics like cotton, linen and silk in acid-free tissue before storing them in cardboard boxes. If they will be hung, slip a cotton pillowcase over them.

4. Mothballs smell yucky and cedar needs an annual sanding, but a lovely smelling moth repellent can be made from a handful of dried lavender or rosemary, a tablespoon of slightly crushed whole cloves and a few shavings of air-dried lemon peel (all found in many natural food stores). Scoop the mixture into hankies or small squares of cotton, tie with narrow lengths of ribbon and toss into drawers, bins and storage boxes to subtly scent clothing and daunt moths.

III. Comatose Storage

Certain possessions are like certain people in our lives—we can't live with 'em, and we can't live without 'em. When we're not yet ready to give up those possessions, there's off-site storage. However, just like hanging on to certain people, we end up paying in the end.

- ⚖ Finding good off-site storage is like finding a good doctor or hairdresser; the best references come from friends and acquaintances. Double-check references with professional movers, since they're familiar with the good, the bad and the ugly of storage facilities.

- ⚖ Make sure the facility has good security, suggests Samantha Scholfield with the California Self Storage Association. Scholfield says good security includes adequate lighting, surveillance cameras, 24/7 staffing and a state-of-the-art lock system.

- ⚖ Give the facility the sniff test before you sign. If it smells damp and musty, it may be a breeding ground for mildew and vermin.

- ⚖ List the contents of your rented unit and keep that list in an easily accessed spot at home. A separate file on "Stored Stuff" is one possibility. Taping the list on the inside door of a kitchen cabinet is another.

- ⚖ Take pictures of each item stored in case anything is stolen or damaged.

- ⚖ Check your homeowner's or renter's insurance policy to see if off-site stored items are covered. If not, determine whether any of that stuff is worth the premium for additional coverage.

⚒ Know that in some states, the entire contents of a unit can legally be sold off if only one month's bill isn't paid.

⚒ Think of off-site storage as limbo for your stuff. Once you let it go, you'll feel a heavenly sense of freedom.

"Souvenirs are perishable; fortunately, memories are not."

—Susan Spano,
The New York Times

LIFE MATTERS:

The Treasure of Friendships

Collect more friends and fewer things. Friends need no packaging, mothballs or insurance and only need storage when they're the out-of-town variety. Besides, when we have friends to keep us happy, we need fewer possessions.

DESIGN FOR LIVING

Playful Storage

When Bill and Melissa Davis bought their colonial-era house in Hingham, Massachusetts, an ugly storage shed marred the view of the woodsy backyard. Not willing to give up the storage space, they replaced the shed with a similar-sized playhouse and painted it to match the main house palette of white with black shutters and a red lacquer door. They even added little window boxes and filled them with the same variety of geraniums and vinca. "We keep all our yard stuff, from snow shovels to fertilizer, there," said Melissa. "You'd never know the building serves such a humble purpose, since it looks like the focal point of the garden."

Bobbi and Gene Hirschkoff of Olivenhain, California, also turned a potential eyesore into an architectural asset with a storage shed constructed to look like a Polynesian hut with bamboo siding and palm-thatched roof. Tucked among palms, ferns and ginger, it looks more like a tropical hideaway than a workaday keeper of a tractor and other yard equipment.

Functional can be fun.

CHAPTER EIGHT

Making Meditative Space

*"Just knowing we have a place we can totally relax
in can get us through times of stress."*

—Carol Venolia, architect

Back in 1956, about the time open floor plans, Elvis Presley and Tom Terrific hit home, more than 100 women sat before a national housing policy hearing and testified that "fewer mothers would end up in mental hospitals or divorce courts if there was one tiny room in the house where they could have peace and quiet without the TV or radio."

A half-century later, that "tiny room" never materialized, yet rooms and noise continue to spill into each other, increasing the stress level for everyone in the household.

The good news is we can have peace and privacy without taking out a mortgage or hauling up to the mountains. We can create it in a corner, a closet or right in our own backyards.

Health practitioner Debbi Graefer did just that when she pitched an eleven-foot square, seven-foot tall tent in the palm grove of her Southern California home.

Dappled with sunlight through its net windows and furnished with shaggy carpeting, a lamp, a tiny table and a couple of draped and padded lounge chairs, it's like a sultan's tent in a shaded oasis. She uses it for meditation, reading, bunking guests and—because the space is so soothing—treating some of her patients.

"Feeling really at home comes with recognizing your needs and learning to satisfy them."
—Joan Kron, *Home Psyche*

"It's one of my favorite spaces, since it's a way of being in nature without being eaten by mosquitoes or exposed to the elements," said Graefer. "And it's so popular with my friends, I let them come and just sit when they need to."

There are scads of simple ways to find peace and privacy for active and passive pursuits. Here are a few of them.

Carve Out Serene Space

❀ Create a reading corner in the bedroom. I found the space for one in my daughter Lisa's old room by hauling a chest of drawers to the closet, moving the bed to a less obvious wall and nestling a comfy chair, an ottoman and a good floor lamp in the corner next to the desk. Draped with a mohair throw and set apart by a thick rug, it's the perfect hideout for a peaceful read.

❀ No room for a chair? Create a cozy nest by throwing down a faux fur rug and some big floor pillows in a sunny spot.

❀ If there's a family room, turn the living room into an "adult retreat." Today's living room is typically open to the front door, making it feel more like an open hallway than the snug space it should be. Sheri Wills of Oceanside, California, gave her wide-open living room a cozier feel by flanking the sofa with a folding screen she fashioned from three hinged sheets of wall-papered plywood. "I've also banned the TV, phone and all other forms of technology from this spot, so no one else in the family seems interested in it," she said. "It's now where I do some of my best thinking and unthinking."

> "Silence is the great teacher, and to learn its lessons you must pay attention to it."
>
> —Deepak Chopra, writer and physician

❀ Make use of that blessed lock, and turn the bathroom into an end-of-the-day sanctuary. Keep a scented candle or two by the tub, and stock a latched cabinet

with fluffy towels, buttery soaps and creamy lotions. Add a terry-covered stool or chair to the room so you can sit and comfortably apply body lotions and creams. A few soothing CDs will drown out the "How long are you going to be in there?" pleas.

❀ Lucky enough to have a window seat? Turn it into a sunlit hideout by hanging curtains, draperies or shades on the outside of the cushion rather than next to the window. Simply pull them shut when you want to be alone.

❀ Move summer indoors. A hammock is at home inside as well as out. When Maribel Vasquez exchanged the bed for a net-draped hammock in her grown-and-gone son's room, she not only made space for an art studio, she also had a place to nap and read. "I love my hammock," said Vasquez. "It not only takes up less space than a bed, but I also don't have to fuss with sheets. It almost feels like I'm on the beach in Brazil again."

❦ Romance the bed. "I've put a lot of energy into my own bed, with a wool mattress on wood slats, topped with off-white flannel sheets," said architect and *Healing Environments* author Carol Venolia. "If you do it right, it's like going home within the home," she said. "Just seeing those fuzzy sheets, pouffy comforter and nice pillows symbolizes clean and nurturing, which does a lot for me."

"If women were convinced that a day off or an hour of solitude was a reasonable ambition they would find a way of attaining it."

—Anne Morrow Lindbergh, writer

❦ Create a cocoon. After a day of slogging through mud and being buffeted by high winds and heavy rain on a hiking tour in the Berkshires, our group of seven each slept in a heavily curtained bed at Blantyre, an elegant inn in Lenox, Massachusetts. We felt so snug in our cozy lairs as the storm howled through the night, we all wanted canopy beds once we got home.

Kids' Hideouts

Kids need cavelike spaces, since they feel dwarfed by big people's furnishings and rooms. They're also less apt to disturb us in our hideouts when they have one of their own.

⚖ Provide a dream house. Ask the manager of an appliance store for a big discarded carton. Encourage a child to make it his or her own by personalizing it with washable markers, stencils and stickers. In his book, *Seinlanguage*, Jerry Seinfeld reminisces that the best toy he ever owned was a refrigerator carton. "This is the closest you're going to come to having your own apartment," he explained. "You can crawl in, 'I'll live here from now on.' Cut a hole in the window, stick your head out. 'Mom, Dad, you must come over some time. We live so close. I'm on the front lawn. It's the Frigidaire building, apartment #1.'"

⚖ Climb a tree. When we moved to our present home years ago, my husband started to build a tree house for our girls in an old eucalyptus at the far end of the property. But with so much to do around the main house, he never got further than building the floor and one wall. Consequently, it wasn't just a tree house, it was a castle, a space ship, a boat and who knows what else. It's good to leave some things to the imagination.

⚖ Sibling squabbles? Curtain a shared room. Sheri Wills installed a ceiling track down the center of her thirteen- and eleven-year-old daughters' bedroom, and hung a floor-length curtain from it. "The privacy issue wasn't such a big deal last year," said Wills. "But now that puberty has hit, it's huge."

> "We need to find God, and he cannot be found in noise and restlessness. God is the friend of silence."
>
> —Mother Teresa

⌂ Add an element of fantasy. I once saw a model home hide-away a kid would trade in his Game Boy for. The designer painted a life-size tree on the wall and cut an irregular, floor-level "squirrel hole" into it that led to a carpeted crawl space behind. "We could have lighted the space," said designer Jim Freeborn. "But we wanted to keep it dark and mysterious. Only flashlights and imagination allowed."

TEN WAYS TO KEEP THE PEACE

With the TV, appliances and other noisemakers, the house can get pretty rackety. A few simple ways to hush them:

1. **Cushion a hardscape.** Surfaces like granite, tile, glass and metal reverberate noise, while softies like upholstery, pillows, draperies and rugs suck it up.

2. **Seek out quiet tools.** A low-tech push mower is not only quieter than its gas-powered cousin, it's also safer, so the job can be delegated to pint-sized assistants. Ditto with an outdoor sweeper like Hoover's SpinSweep, a kind of carpet sweeper for the yard that's a peaceful alternative to an earsplitting leaf blower.

3. **Soften the slam.** Glue small silicone bumpers to the upper and lower corners of cabinet doors. Cork-lined kitchen drawers will also cut the clatter.

4. **Tame the phone.** Turn down the ringer, mute the answering machine and return messages when you have the time and the will. Whether it's mobile or stationary, remember that a phone is there for *your* convenience, not everyone else's.

5. **Mute the computer.** Does anyone really need to hear that crackle and whistle of the Web connection? Crank up the volume only when active listening is necessary.

6. **Caulk a crack.** Keep noise as well as dust, heat and cold from creeping through cracks by filling gaps around window and door seals.

7. **Invest in headphones that tune into the TV.** A good accessory when your partner wants Leno and you want your zzz's.

8. **Catch a breeze.** The whoosh of an electric fan masks a racket, and its rhythmic hum can lull you into a restful state. Or check out a sound machine—with a flip of a switch, it replicates bird song, breaking waves or a summer thunderstorm.

9. **Add water.** A splashing fountain in the garden or a gurgling aquarium in the bedroom is a pretty way to drown the din.

10. **Mix in music.** Make note of what relaxes, and create a library of calming CDs and tapes. I've found some of the most soothing sounds at New Age bookstores, but anything from Brahms to Nora Jones will do as long as it peacefully screens what you don't want to hear.

Inner Escapes

Creating a hideout at home just takes a little imagination, but creating a hideout in our heads takes practice and dedication.

I've long struggled with the discipline of meditation, yet whether or not I can quiet my monkey mind and sink into a state of peace, just closing my eyes and sitting quietly for a few minutes in the morning puts me in a better place. I must admit, however, that I can go for weeks without even thinking to meditate.

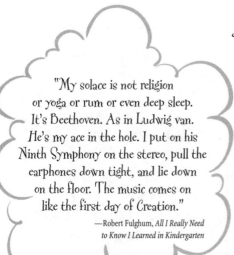

"My solace is not religion or yoga or rum or even deep sleep. It's Beethoven. As in Ludwig van. He's my ace in the hole. I put on his Ninth Symphony on the stereo, pull the earphones down tight, and lie down on the floor. The music comes on like the first day of Creation."

—Robert Fulghum, *All I Really Need to Know I Learned in Kindergarten*

"Most of us are so busy on the outside, we don't take the time to be quiet and see what's going on within," said psychotherapist and meditation teacher Gita Morena at the Inshallah Retreat Center in El Cajon, California. She suggests the following steps to make meditation a natural part of day-to-day living.

- **Create a reminder.** When Morena first faced the challenge of incorporating meditation into her busy day, she'd toss a cushion in the middle of the floor and think, "I want to be meditating there." She said, "That cushion finally seduced me into a regular practice."

- **Initiate a ritual.** Lighting a candle, burning incense or tuning in to special music can be a signal to the mind that it's about to enter inner space.

- **Take it gradually.** According to Morena, it doesn't matter whether we sit for thirty seconds or thirty minutes; the more we do, the more we'll eventually want to do.

- **Align the spine.** The straighter we sit, the better energy flows through the body to the mind. "It may be uncomfortable at first," explains Morena. "But a little discomfort can keep us awake and aware."

❦ **Still the mind by focusing on the breath.** "Quieting the mind is often the hardest part, since we all suffer from invading thoughts," said Morena. "But just watching our thoughts surface, then bringing them back to where they started, is a constant, calming process."

> "In solitude we give passionate attention to our lives, to our memories, to the details around us."
>
> —Virginia Woolf,
> *A Room of One's Own*

❦ **Consider a teacher.** "A meditation teacher can't make the trip for you, but he or she can guide you through the territory when you're stuck or scared," said Morena. "It's the best way to go deeper into your practice."

Weaving Mini Meditations into the Day

"When meditation is integrated into all aspects of your life, it disappears, but your life becomes permanently enriched," wrote Zen practitioner Gary Thorpe in *Sweeping Changes*. Some ways to do so:

⚐ Instead of standing or sitting at a table while tackling normally stationary chores, consider doing them in a porch swing or rocking chair. There's something inherently meditative about shucking peas or sewing a hem while rocking, especially if it's on a porch or by an open window on a pleasant day.

⚐ After a sedentary workday, appreciate the sensations of stretching to dust a shelf and bending to scrub a floor. Contemplate how the clearing of dust, dirt and debris serves as a metaphor for clearing the habits and addictions that muck up life.

⚞ Be mindful. When we're fully aware of even our smallest actions, we'll always know where we've set down our glasses, stashed that important paper or turned off the burner under the chili. In other words, live in the moment and savor its details. "Be where you are," advised the Buddha. "Otherwise, you will miss most of your life."

> "Nothing can bring you peace but yourself."
>
> —Ralph Waldo Emerson

Get Away from It All

It's good to escape the cacophony of civilization every so often, and it can be as simple as pitching a tent in the woods or checking into a retreat center for the weekend. My husband and I took a more indulgent route recently when we spent a week at Kona Village, a Hawaiian resort that has no TV, radio or phone in its thatched-roof huts.

The first couple of days without CNN, Terry Gross and voicemail can be rough on a technojunkie, but eventually one becomes aware of the natural world: birdsong, rain on the roof, the fragrance of cut grass. Nature has the power to fill the unplugged void and resuscitate even the most stressed soul.

Take a Day Off at Home

Real getaways are great when you can get them, but every so often I take a vacation that requires no packing, no security lines, no jet lag, no recovery time and minimal money. In short, I take an inner journey at home. Like a real trip, planning an in-home getaway is almost as much fun as taking it, so the day before, I do errands and clear my schedule so I won't need to drive the car, get into the computer, make phone calls or all the other things I generally have to do.

> "In order to give back to our relationships, careers, families, and passions, we must pull in for short moments to take care of ourselves . . ."
>
> —Chris Casson Madden,
> design writer

I also:

- ❀ Schedule all I *want* to do the following day, like nap, putter and read. A list isn't necessary, but the structure of it gives me a sense of security when a free day stretches out before me.

- ❀ Stack a pile of lifestyle magazines and a juicy book by my reading nest.

- ❀ Stock up on a slew of fresh fruit and veggies, and assemble three or four simple, light meals.

On retreat day, I:

- ❀ Get up at dawn to watch the sky change color and hear the birds chatter as they wake.

- ❀ Meditate.

- ❀ Have my morning coffee out on the patio. Even if it's rainy or cold, I dress for the weather, sit in a sheltered spot  and become aware of the sounds and smells around me. I find that when I feel connected to the world outside, I can better connect to the world within.

❀ Keep off the TV, radio and other disturbers of the peace.

❀ Mute the phone ringer and let the answering machine pick up all messages. Since my family knows what I'm up to, no one freaks when I'm unavailable for the day.

❀ Enjoy the weather. If the day is pleasant, I wear something light and gauzy, open all the windows and let the sun shine in. If it's cold and dark, I wear something warm, light a candle and build a fire in the fireplace.

> "We learn about others when we're with them. When we're alone we discover things about ourselves."
>
> —Alexandra Stoddard

I also:

❀ Slather my face with a mix of mashed avocado (from my planned omelet) and aloe vera (from the plant on my windowsill) for an all-day facial mask. I may look like the Hulk today, but tomorrow I'll glow.

 ❀ Brush and massage about a teaspoon of olive oil in my hair for deep conditioning, then don a baseball cap to naturally warm it. The cap also keeps me from scaring myself in the mirror.

❀ Forget my watch. There are clocks in the house, but the act of not wearing a watch symbolizes that time doesn't count today.

❀ Do an enjoyable project I've been putting off, like sketching, organizing a drawer full of recipes or pasting pictures of coveted rooms and gardens into my dream-house book.

❀ Go for a long walk, preferably well away from traffic. The nearby beach or trails do it for me. I also like to walk where I can get a treat, like a nonfat latte and chocolate biscotti—something that won't dent the day's diet.

❀ Soak my feet in warm water, rub in an exfoliating cream, trim my toenails and paint them silvery pink.

❀ Read or nap in the hammock—partly to let my toes dry in the breeze.

❀ Have dinner, preferably outside, while watching the sky darken.

❀ Rinse off the mask, slather on face cream and sink into a warm, fragrant bath while the cream sinks into my warm, still greenish skin.

❀ Massage body lotion all over after emerging from the bath and toweling off.

❀ Crawl into bed early, paint my fingernails (they're less likely to smudge in bed), give thanks for the day and read till I drop off into dreamland.

"Meditation is a major pathway to the soul."

—Elaine Saint James, *Inner Simplicity*

I've found this day of indulgent solitude not only restorative but eventually productive. It's like scattering a mix of unidentifiable seeds in my garden. I never know what's going to emerge, but sometimes it's something fruitful.

DESIGN FOR LIVING

Create a Sleeping Alcove

While remodeling our house a few years ago, we decided that we'd get more mileage out of our guest-room by moving the bed from the middle of the room and making a niche for it against a wall, free-ing the rest of the space for a desk and a comfort-able chair. So off came the closet sliding doors and in went the mattress and box springs that we cov-ered to look like a sofa—back cushions and all. Two narrow closets now flank the bed, and soft fabric over batting is stapled to the wall behind it. For back-to-the-womb warmth, I hung matching drapery panels around the bed to close off the world when needed. It's the perfect place to hide out with a good read and a small stash of chocolate.

LIFE MATTERS:

Find Meaning in Cleaning

It helps to understand the deeper meaning of chores by focusing on the benefits rather than the bother. When cooking a meal, for example, meditate on how that food will nourish and please those you love. When scrubbing a tub, imagine how smooth the porcelain will feel as you sink your weary body into the suds. When washing sheets, think how fresh they'll smell as you drift off to sleep. Visualize the reward and then revel in it.

CHAPTER NINE

Let There Be Light

"In the right light, at the right time,
everything is extraordinary."

—Arron Rose, writer

In the beginning, there was light. People worked and played in it, took comfort in it and worshiped it. They even cleaned in it. But since it felt so good to be in the light, a little dust and disarray didn't seem like such a big deal. And it was good.

"Where the sun does not enter, the doctor does."

—Italian proverb

Over time, people learned to manipulate light so they could bring out the best in themselves and their surroundings. Some of those skills were forgotten with the advent of the fluorescent bulb and flat, uniform lighting, but fortunately, many of them have come to light again.

Follow the Sun

☼ If you have the luxury of building or remodeling, orient rooms to the sun's path. "We're at our best," said architect and *Healing Environments* author Carol Venolia, "when we awaken in the East light, carry out our main activities in the South light, then rest at the end of the day in the West or North light."

✿ Be mobile. "I tend to push furnishings, like the kitchen table and the sofa, near the windows so that I get the most from the aesthetic and biological benefits of light," said Venolia. "You can also see better in natural rather than artificial light."

✿ Make sun-seeking easy by attaching casters to large furnishings. We have a couple of easy chairs on casters that sit in front of the den fireplace by night but can be rolled to the windows by day when we want to read or simply sit in the sun.

✿ Draw natural light into a room's dark corners by hanging a few well-placed mirrors. We recently painted our bedroom walls russet red—a rich look, with a back-to-the-womb feel. But the color absorbs much of the natural light. I remedied the situation by hanging a small sunburst mirror on the wall adjacent to the north-facing window so it reflects the west-setting sun. I hung a larger, rectangular mirror on the wall opposite the south window so that it reflects the view of the walled garden and brightens the corner. The room is still cozily dramatic but no longer cavelike.

> "If we bring light into a dark room, the darkness disappears, and inasmuch as a soul is filled with good, evil disappears."
>
> —Shaker proverb

✿ Borrow light from an adjacent room.
Chicago building designer Tom Watson did just that when he

READER/CUSTOMER CARE SURVEY

HEFG

We care about your opinions! Please take a moment to fill out our online Reader Survey at **http://survey.hcibooks.com**. As a **"THANK YOU"** you will receive a **VALUABLE INSTANT COUPON** towards future book purchases as well as a **SPECIAL GIFT** available only online! Or, you may mail this card back to us and we will send you a copy of our exciting catalog with your valuable coupon inside.
(PLEASE PRINT IN ALL CAPS)

First Name		MI.		Last Name	

Address				City	

State	Zip		Email		

1. Gender
- ☐ Female ☐ Male

2. Age
- ☐ 8 or younger
- ☐ 9-12 ☐ 13-16
- ☐ 17-20 ☐ 21-30
- ☐ 31+

3. Did you receive this book as a gift?
- ☐ Yes ☐ No

4. Annual Household Income
- ☐ under $25,000
- ☐ $25,000 - $34,999
- ☐ $35,000 - $49,999
- ☐ $50,000 - $74,999
- ☐ over $75,000

5. What are the ages of the children living in your house?
- ☐ 0 - 14 ☐ 15+

6. Marital Status
- ☐ Single
- ☐ Married
- ☐ Divorced
- ☐ Widowed

7. How did you find out about the book?
(please choose one)
- ☐ Recommendation
- ☐ Store Display
- ☐ Online
- ☐ Catalog/Mailing
- ☐ Interview/Review

8. Where do you usually buy books?
(please choose one)
- ☐ Bookstore
- ☐ Online
- ☐ Book Club/Mail Order
- ☐ Price Club (Sam's Club, Costco's, etc.)
- ☐ Retail Store (Target, Wal-Mart, etc.)

9. What subject do you enjoy reading about the most?
(please choose one)
- ☐ Parenting/Family
- ☐ Relationships
- ☐ Recovery/Addictions
- ☐ Health/Nutrition
- ☐ Christianity
- ☐ Spirituality/Inspiration
- ☐ Business Self-help
- ☐ Women's Issues
- ☐ Sports

10. What attracts you most to a book?
(please choose one)
- ☐ Title
- ☐ Cover Design
- ☐ Author
- ☐ Content

TAPE IN MIDDLE; DO NOT STAPLE

BUSINESS REPLY MAIL
FIRST-CLASS MAIL PERMIT NO 45 DEERFIELD BEACH, FL

POSTAGE WILL BE PAID BY ADDRESSEE

Health Communications, Inc.
3201 SW 15th Street
Deerfield Beach FL 33442-9875

FOLD HERE

Comments

cut three 12" square openings high in the wall between a client's sunny living room and a dark hallway. "The high 'windows' not only brighten things up, the borrowed light makes the narrow hallway seem wider," explained Watson.

✿ Consider the French door. Homes built before World War II often used interior glass doors between public rooms to spread light while providing a sense of separation.

> "A day without sunshine is like, you know, night."
>
> —Southern California bumper sticker

✿ Fake it. Tom Watson installed narrow, warm, white fluorescent tubes in the deep window wells between his interior shutters and the window glass in his own apartment. "They give the effect of sunlight streaming through the blades, even on the city's dreariest days," said Watson. "I'd rather have sunshine, but when the weather stinks, the tubes help."

✿ Open up to the sun by installing a skylight in a bathroom or over the kitchen island. Bodies and towels will dry faster, makeup and shaving will be more accurate, cooking will be pleasanter and electric bills will be lower.

LOVE IN THE LIGHT

According to science writer Marc McCutcheon in *The Compass in Your Nose,* the best time for lovemaking is not in the dark of night but in the full light of day.

McCutcheon states that sunlight arouses sex drive by stimulating the pituitary gland, which regulates the ovaries and testes. Darkness, on the other hand, signals the pineal gland to produce hormones that inhibit ovulation, sperm count and sex drive.

Light Cleaning

❀ Clear the windows of overgrown vegetation. Years ago, when the real estate market was down, we looked for an investment property that we could rent out for a few years, then sell when  the market warmed up. We found a cute little house in a great location, but the inside was dark and dreary. It didn't take long to figure out why. A curtain of bamboo and twisted junipers had grown in front of most of the windows, darkening the rooms. It took some time to hack through the overgrowth. Once we did, light flooded into the house; and after a little paint and a lot of polish, so did the tenants. The new buyer liked it, he said, because "It felt so cheerful."

❀ Seeing through a glass darkly? Dust and grease from within a home and air pollution from without leave a gray film on windows. "The residue of pollen and smoke are not always easy to see," said window washer Mark Garnier. "But once those panes are polished, it's surprising how bright rooms become." Garnier's route to a quick shine is with a solution of 6 tablespoons of ammonia mixed with warm water in a 26-ounce spray bottle, polished off with a wad of newspaper. Windows, he said, are best washed on a cloudy day, since sunlight makes any cleaning solution streak. Besides, aren't there better things to do when the sun shines?

❀ Make use of the sun's natural germicidal powers the way our ancestors did by airing rugs, bedding, seat cushions and stored clothing outdoors on the first warm, sunny day of spring.

❀ Most furnishings will die of old age, abuse or boredom before the sun destroys them, but precious photos and art should be framed with UV-filtering glass and kept out of direct sunlight. It's also smart to occasionally rearrange furnishings that are exposed to sun so they fade evenly.

❀ Furnish with machine-washable whites. White comforters, curtains, towels and even slipcovers can brighten a room without burdening the room keeper if fabrics can be washed and bleached.

> "Good lighting meets your needs, puts you at ease, creates a sense of comfort, blends into the background and enhances the colors, forms and textures of the furnishings in a room."
>
> —Lisa Skolnik, *The Right Light*

❀ Color the walls clean and cozy. Pure white walls have a crisp, pristine look and reflect the most light. They can also have a chilling effect, as we discovered when we painted our rental home's interior. A second coat of cream warmed things up without compromising brightness.

Light Decorating

✿ Consider the woodwork. The walls may be white, but darkly stained doors, headboards and wall moldings suck up a good bit of light and can add gloom to a room. When it comes time for a redo, think about a whitewash.

✿ Create everyday sunshine by painting a ceiling yellow. The room will seem to glow from above.

✿ If privacy isn't a problem, consider hanging transparent or translucent curtains at the window. Peach, yellow or rose colored sheers work wonders at warming cool northern light. They're also good for hiding smudges and fingerprints on window glass. Another good option is shutters, provided they have wide blades and a glossy (read: low-maintenance) finish. Shutters not only mask smudges, they also provide privacy and fine-tune light rather than block it—and they're easier to clean than window blinds.

> "Moonlight is sculpture. Sunlight is painting."
> —Nathaniel Hawthorne

EARLY BIRD OR NIGHT OWL?

Studies indicate that morning people prefer bright, even light, translucent window coverings and light, clear colors in their surroundings.

Those who peak at night, however, are happiest with an artful contrast of light and shade, industrial-strength blackout shades and deep rich colors on the walls.

Night Brighteners

❀ Provide a lamp for every seat. "Two things most people never seem to have enough of are lamps and plants," said Marie Kinnaman, a Fallbrook, California interior designer, who often appears on HGTV's *Decorating Cents*. "Even if a room is lit from a ceiling fixture above, lamps give it a much warmer feeling and make it more functional."

✿ Just as the eye loves dappled sunlight outdoors, it craves a soft contrast of light and shadow indoors. Create golden pools of light with opaque lampshades on chandeliers and on all but reading lamps. Shades also direct light to a table below.

✿ Create a human scale under a high ceiling by hanging wall sconces just above eye level. I've avoided trauma to both walls and wallet by using glass-enclosed candle sconces instead of electric sconces. The flickering effect of candles is soft and romantic, and the placement of the sconces gives the tall room a more human scale.

✿ Saddled with outdated track lighting? Design writer Lisa Skolnik suggests either updating those old tracks with new fixtures or varying the fixtures on the track. "They don't have to be the same," she writes in her book *The Right Light*. "It can be both interesting and effective to mix spotlights and floodlights to create varying pools and points of light."

> "Uniform illumination— the sweetheart of lighting engineers—serves no useful purpose whatsoever. In fact, it destroys the social nature of the space, and makes people feel disoriented and unbounded."
>
> —Christopher Alexander, *A Pattern Language*

✿ Vary the intensity of light on table and floor lamps as well—a 25-watt bulb here, a 75-watt there, with as many of them as possible on dimmers. Variety creates versatility as well as visual interest.

❀ The higher the wattage, the colder the light. The lower the wattage, the mellower the light. Better to have more lamps with lower wattage than the other way around.

❀ Manage the mood. Turn up the lights when there are chores to be done. Switch to mellow levels when it's time to relax.

❀ Spotlight a favorite wall-hung picture or two. When there's no time or energy to clean, turn down the rest of the lights and give the eye something besides dust and disorder to take in. Selective lighting can throw guilt in the dark.

Working Light

✿ Remedy a dimly lit bathroom by placing a slender gooseneck lamp on the counter. Tweezing, shaving and reading medicine labels require bright light, and a gooseneck lamp can easily direct it. Make sure to use a standard, silvered incandescent bulb, since it imitates daylight better than its cooler fluorescent cousin.

✿ Hard-to-reach sockets? Screw compact fluorescent bulbs into high ceiling fixtures and other out-of-the-way spots. Compact fluorescent bulbs fit into standard outlets, give a warmer glow than conventional fluorescent bulbs and have amazingly long life spans.

✿ Choose a wall-mounted, swing-arm lamp to light a desk or a reading area. Unlike table lamps that have to be moved to clean the spot where they sit, a wall-mounted lamp keeps a table and desk free and clear. Once I replaced the table lamp on my chair-side reading table with a wall-hung, swing-arm lamp, I found I could stack another pile of books and still have space for my mug, my water glass, and my pen and pencil holder.

✿ Whether it's a wall-hung, table or floor model, position a lamp so that a right-hander has light spilling over his or her left shoulder and a lefty has it coming from the right.

> "Let the light that shines brightly inside you become the light that guides the energy of your home."
>
> —Alexandra Stoddard

✿ Prevent glare by placing a lamp about two feet from reading material with the bottom of the shade no higher than eye level.

✿ A translucent shade with a wide bottom is best for reading and writing, since it spills a generous arc of light across a page and beyond. Dark shades are good for dramatic effect, but the circle of light they cast is so crisp, it can cause eyestrain while reading.

✿ Too much light before bedtime may delay and disturb sleep, especially with children. Better to gradually dim the lights in the evening before turning in.

✿ Stumbling in the dark? Plug photocell nightlights into hallway and bathroom outlets. Like creatures of the night, these light-sensitive bulbs turn themselves on at dusk and off at dawn.

Special Effects

❀ Hang a panel of stained glass in a sunny window. Architects of the great cathedrals of medieval Europe believed that light shining through certain colors, particularly violet and cobalt blue, increased contemplative powers and kindled one's "inner light."

❀ Place prisms, geodes and crystal objects near a window to refract and scatter bits of light on walls and ceilings. Light takes on many forms, and when it's faceted, it's glorious.

❀ Hang a glass shelf or two across a sunny window, and fill it with jewel-toned glass bottles or vases. The sun will cast jewel-toned shadows around the room.

❀ Position silver, crystal and brass objects so they sparkle in sunlight and glow in lamp and candlelight.

❀ Cast leafy patterns on the walls by poking an up-light for plants in the soil of a large potted plant. I've stuck one between two pots of philodendron that sit at the base of a big ficus in my living room. The plant hides the fixture and throws its own heart-shaped shadows on the surrounding walls.

❀ Quell a child's fear of the dark by softly illuminating a favorite picture or toy with a low-voltage accent light. Or create your own night sky with a glow-in-the-dark universe. After eight-year-old Tyler Gould caught the planetarium show at San Diego's Fleet Space Theater, he had to have a few packages of the self-sticking stars from the museum shop, which his mom applied to the ceiling above his bed.

"You can't really see them till it gets dark," said his mother Natalie. "So the dark isn't so scary anymore."

❧ Candlelight flatters food and faces, so use it often. The circa 1760 Old Inn on the Green in New Marlborough, Massachusetts, illuminates its four dining rooms, tap room and terrace exclusively in candlelight. Placed on tables and sideboards, in chandeliers and on windowsills, the dripless candles cast a romantic, old-world glow no bulb can match.

> "There are two ways of spreading the light: to be the candle or the light that reflects it."
> —Edith Wharton, writer

❧ Make a hurricane lamp or votive holder easier to clean by adding a bit of water to its base before inserting the candle.

Outdoor Lightscaping

A little creative lightscaping in the yard can create outdoor living in warm weather and year-round night views from inside. It can also add safety and security better and prettier than prison-yard floodlights.

𝒫 Create an outdoor room by treating perimeter plantings as walls and the undersides of large trees as ceilings, softly bathing them in light. Highlight special features, like flowerbeds, a fountain or a specimen tree.

𝒫 Spotlighting a tree? Highlight fall foliage by replacing a standard white bulb with a red or yellow one.

𝒫 Keep it subtle. A little light goes a long way in the great outdoors.

🖊 The main idea behind landscape lighting is to play up the good and ignore the bad. When lighting is carefully planned, we won't see those scraggly shrubs, aphid-eaten roses or the crabgrass in the lawn. Instead, we'll only focus on what we want to see. If only we could light our lives that way.

> "Arise, shine:
> for your light
> has come."
> —Isaiah 60:1

DESIGN FOR LIVING

Turn an Everyday Yard into a Nighttime Fantasy

Stock up on holiday candles and mini-lights in late fall and early winter for parties in the summer. I recently attended an afternoon wedding that turned into a midsummer's night dream with imaginative, though simple, lighting. The bride's family wove dark green strands of hundreds of white mini-lights around an arbor and through the pepper trees in the yard. In addition to placing candles in hurricane lamps on the tables, they also created a ribbon of light by outlining the curving paths of the garden with luminaria—white paper lunch bags filled with sand-anchored votive candles. The whole effect was festive and magical.

LIFE MATTERS:

Celebrate the Solstice

The ancients, who were so closely tied to the sun and its sustenance, honored the Earth's cycles of light. Today more of us are beginning to do the same, since the first day of summer and winter are benchmarks for the year.

At the Inshallah Retreat in El Cajon, California, psychotherapist and meditation teacher Gita Morena celebrates the winter solstice by gathering approximately two dozen people in a circle for an evening of meditation, prayer and sharing. Sometimes she'll place a stack of Zen tarot cards in the center of the circle and have each participant draw from it. Other times she'll have each person light a votive candle and place it on a center tray, so that in the course of the evening, the candles melt into one.

"Our evening of winter solstice is all about going within, to that place of darkness, and bringing consciousness to it," said Morena. "We focus on what we're ready to let go of and the intentions we'll plant. It's all about giving birth to the light within."

In the summer, Morena creates a similar circle ritual, but this time she focuses on developing intentions, the quality of the harvest and reaping the good of what has been sown in the soul.

"This is the time of year we begin to weed our gardens," said Morena. "So we discuss what we're weeding from our lives and what we'll cultivate for the rest of the year."

"Celebrating the solstice helps us pay attention to what's happening around us through the year," said Morena. "It's a good way to align ourselves with that energy."

Whether we do something as simple as lighting a candle on the darkest night of winter or as interesting as attending a weekend summer solstice celebration, connecting with the seasons of dark and light reminds us of nature's continual ebb and flow.

CHAPTER TEN

The Tao of Dust

*"The dust bunnies that skulk beneath the couch
and behind the refrigerator contain everything from
space diamonds to Saharan dust to the bones of
dinosaurs and bits of modern tire rubber."*

—Hannah Holmes, *The Secret Life of Dust*

Dust gets around. Great clouds of it continually rise from the earth, sail on the wind, seep through our windows and settle within. Yet much of what we chase down and sweep up in our homes is simply bits of ourselves, since we shed skin at about 40,000 microscopic flakes a minute.

We emit so much of this stuff, some museums and historic sites have taken to "bathing" people before allowing entry to their inner sanctums. Even before the *Da Vinci Code* made *The Last Supper* Milan's hot spot, visitors have had to pass through two separate chambers that electronically suck out the dead skin and hitchhiking sulfuric acid, sulfur dioxide and pesticides that make up the human aura.

> "For dust
> thou art, and
> unto dust shalt
> thou return."
> —Genesis 3:19

No one has figured out how to automatically eradicate dust from our own inner sanctums, however—though one woman has come close. Frances Gabe, an inventor in Newberg, Oregon, designed a house for herself with a carwash-like system that washes, rinses and blow-dries everything in it from its waterproof furnishings to its heavily varnished wood floors. A drain in the fireplace carries away ashes to fertilize the yard, a section of the closet cleans the clothes, the kitchen cabinets wash and dry the dishes, and a chute carries out the trash.

Still dust exists, even in the Gabe house. While we can't eradicate it, there are ways to minimize it in our homes and save ourselves a good bit of time, energy and maybe even our health in the process.

Outwit Incoming Dust

❀ Choose your neighborhood. As they say in real estate, the three most important factors when choosing a home are location, location and location. So besides proximity to a good

school or pizzeria, check out the downwind location of a dust-generating highway, farm or factory. Growing up outside of Boston, my family's home was about halfway between a soap factory and a sulfur pit. Our household dust was not only abundant, it was chemically charged. Fortunately, the house was set on a knoll; lower-sited houses sucked in even more of the stuff.

❀ Close the windows on bad air days. San Diego is blessed with a near perfect climate and decent air quality, so most residents practice an open window policy much of the year. But after the devastating wild fires of October 2003, when over 2,500 homes and hundreds of thousands of acres burned, a fine layer of soot made its way through open windows throughout the county for weeks, forcing survivors to button up. The air quality has returned to its normal levels, but now that windows are open again, more of us are newly attuned to how much dust regularly drifts in during the day, especially when it's windy or smoggy.

❀ Apply weather stripping to all windows and doors, and caulk all cracks. Stripping and caulking not only keep dust from seeping in but also keep hot and frigid air out.

> "Every particle of dust is a particle of danger. Never forget this, and you will save yourself much trouble and grief."
> —An experienced housewife (1893),
> *Mangles, Mops and Feather Brushes*

❀ Change or wash heating and air conditioner filters seasonally. Filters get grungy fast, especially in extreme temperatures. If they're washable, toss them in the dishwasher for a good scrub without the elbow grease.

❀ Consider replacing an ordinary fiberglass filter in a central cooling and heating unit with a media, electronic or HEPA (high-efficiency particulate-arresting) filter. All three filters effectively trap the tiniest particles of airborne dust, pollen and even smoke, so they don't settle on surfaces. If you lack a whole-house unit, consider a portable air cleaner for individual rooms.

Diminish Homemade Dust

⌂ Flip on the stove fan to suck up grease when cooking. When dust mixes with cooking oil, it turns into kitchen-coating sludge.

⌂ Avoid humidifiers, especially if the local water supply is hard. The fine white dust from minerals not only leaves its telltale mark, it can also damage computers and other electronic equipment.

> "Nature abhors a vacuum. And so do I."
> —Anne Gibbons, cartoonist

⌂ Shed the shoes. According to test labs at the Hoover Company, the average rug is embedded with two pounds of dust, much of which has been tracked in on footwear. Shoe shucking is a fairly easy habit to establish, if there's a place to both change and store them. Interior designer Joyce Yamada placed a padded bench in her garage for easy shoe removal and storage. She also outfitted a long, low cabinet/seat with shelves for shoes and baskets for slipper socks in her foyer. "The easier you make shoe removal, the more it's going to happen," said Joyce. "Even the kids' friends, who are used to wearing shoes in their own homes, kick them off here when they see our boys doing it."

> "Wearing shoes in the house was barbaric. There was almost as much indignity in wearing shoes in the house as there was in being kidnapped."
> —Ann Patchett, author, Bel Canto

⌂ Keep a good-sized, rough-surfaced mat just outside each door. I have mats with a perforated scroll design that allows shuffled dirt and dust to drop through the openings to the pavement below. Consequently, there's no hard-to-clean buildup that makes its way inside. The Carpet and Rug Institute recommends going one step further by laying a soft, absorbent mat just inside each door to sop up remaining muck.

    ⌣ Keep Rover groomed. Better to bathe and brush the dog than to hunt down and suck up his dander, hair and whatever he's just rolled in.

⌣ Cultivate indoor greenery. Researchers at Washington State University have found that houseplants, particularly Boston ferns, English ivy, palms and chrysanthemums, clean the air of airborne dust, molds and bacteria.

⌣ Avoid the fake and the dead. Dried and "silk" plants and flowers are dust magnets. Life is too short to dust a fake philodendron.

> "I am no longer aware of dust. I have shed my Puritan conscience about absolute tidiness and cleanliness."
>
> —Anne Morrow Lindbergh

Shed Dust Like a Duck

❀ Paint high gloss enamel on windowsills, so dust doesn't settle. It's also a good idea to rub a little floor wax into the tracks of sliding glass windows and doors to keep those grooves gunk-free.

❀ Seal the garage floor with either a clear concrete sealer or a colored epoxy to keep dust down
and make the floor easier to sweep. We had our
garage floor covered in a cream, tan, gray and black
splattered epoxy that not only sheds dust and dirt, it
disguises it beautifully.

❀ Wax wood. An annual or biannual (depending on how
often the piece is used) application of paste wax on a wood
surface makes it too slick for dust to stick. Waxed wood also
has a rich, deep luster that only needs a swift swipe of a soft
cloth to keep its glow. "Just avoid killing a piece with care,"
advises Antony Buxton, a conservator of fine furniture and
lecturer at England's Oxford University Department for
Continuing Education. "People often complain that their furniture is greasy, which is usually the result of constantly applying wax," he said. For week-to-week maintenance, Buxton
advises dusting waxed wood with a wax-impregnated cloth.

❀ A good sheen comes from lots of buffing, not gobs of wax.
After applying wax, wait 20 minutes for it to absorb into the
wood, advises Buxton. Then use plenty of arm-toning elbow
grease, rubbing in the direction of the grain.

❀ Since solvents in a good paste wax soften earlier applications,
old layers of wax slough off in the buffing process. But if a
piece is truly grimy, Buxton advises stripping the surface with
a chamois firmly wrung out in a mixture of one egg cup (about
2½ tablespoons) of white vinegar to one pint of warm water,
then buffing it with a soft, clean cloth. "This 'conservator's
recipe' is very good at removing dirt, dust and fingerprints, and

leaves a fine hard shine," explained Buxton. "As my Italian maestro in Florence used to say of furniture restoration, '*Chi vuole il mistero,* Tony.' It's all a great mystery."

❀ Fear of waxy buildup? Fahhgedaboutit. It's an old Madison Avenue ploy to sell us the spray-on stuff. Unless a surface is gunky (in which case it'll have to be stripped with the vinegar-water recipe) solvents in a good paste wax soften the earlier layer of wax, which sloughs off in the buffing process.

> "We live in a world where lemonade is made from artificial flavors and furniture polish is made with real lemons."
>
> —Alfred E. Newman
> *Mad* magazine

❀ Avoid dust-attracting oils and silicone from spray-on products. In fact, it's critical to avoid silicone and oil on wax, since they can leave a gummy, dull, dust-attracting film that damages wood over time.

THE BEAUTY OF DUST

When the British National Trust acquired Chastleton House, a 400-year-old manor home in the English Cotswolds, birds lived in the attic, water dripped from the walls, and blankets of dust and cobwebs grew thick on tables, chests and chairs. The last private owner, Mrs. Barbara Clutten-Brook, excused the dust as a way to "accentuate the contours of the furniture." And the cobwebs? "They should always be retained," sniffed the widow. "As they hold the place together."

Decorative Dust Deflectors

⊿ **Leather upholstery:** It sheds dust like a slicker sheds rain. Go for an aged bomber jacket look, and it'll camouflage wear as well.

⊿ **Glass doors:** Take a tip from Tiffany's and keep glassware, china and other pretty stuff on dust-free display. It's easier to keep a pane or two pristine than the cache of collectibles behind them.

> "After the first four years the dirt doesn't get any worse."
> —Quentin Crisp, writer

⊿ **Hard surfaced flooring:** Dust burrows deep into wall-to-wall carpeting. When the carpeting gives up the ghost, consider replacing at least some of it with wood, stone or tile. Many allergy sufferers have done just that and find both the dust levels and sniffles lessened.

⊿ **Outdoor table coverings:** A patio table can be kept clean by covering it with a plastic or fabric tablecloth weighed down with stones. When it's time to dine, simply whisk off the cover and replace it with a fresh cloth, or dine on the bare surface below.

⊿ **Dusty tones:** When choosing fabric, paints and woods, lean toward grayed colors, like sage green, Wedgwood blue, dusty rose, mauve and taupe—they'll show less dust than clearer colors.

⊿ **Matte finishes:** Selecting a matte finish over a glossy one will hide the inevitable. A low-luster teak table, for instance, will camouflage dust better than a shiny mahogany or glass-topped one.

AVOID DUST CATCHERS

Pleated lampshades, elaborately carved wood, tufted upholstery and fussy window treatments attract and trap dust in their pleats, crevices and folds. If you want to deal with less dust, stick to simple and streamlined shapes and designs.

Six Dust Delinquents and How to Reform Them

"Excuse my dust."
—Dorothy Parker's requested epitaph

1. **An unplanted yard:** Whether it's a tiny patch of bare earth by the front door or a fallow field out back, plant it, mulch it or pave it. Otherwise, billions of bits of it will make their way inside. "It took us two and a half years to afford to landscape the backyard of our new house," said Diane Lindstrom of Poway, California. "But once the sod and patio were in, we noticed an immediate decrease in the cleaning we had to do."

2. **Dirty ducts:** Air ducts get grungy in time, especially after any sort of construction. Our heating ducts were so caked with crud after a whole house remodeling, we shuddered at the sight of what came out of them—gunk we had been inhaling for months. The first indication of dirty ducts is a fried dust odor when the heater or air conditioner is switched on. When that happens, call in a pro. Amateur duct cleaning is akin to amateur angioplasty.

3. **A full vacuum bag:** A bursting bag can disperse more dust through a room than it sucks up, so make sure it's secured

tightly and change it when it's about three-quarters full. When I purchased my last vacuum cleaner, I researched what looked like a winner—a bagless model. But after reading *Consumer Reports,* I found that the bin that substitutes for a bag has to be emptied more frequently, and emptying it can kick up a cloud of dust.

4. **Fireplaces:** All wood-burning fireplaces emit some sort of air-borne soot, but this can be reduced by burning well-seasoned hardwoods like oak, hickory and eucalyptus, rather than softwood evergreens and pressed-wood packaged logs. Have the chimney inspected for blockages and creosote buildup every so often to keep the place from burning down—the ultimate dust maker.

5. **Candles:** All candles, including smokeless types, increase dust levels to some degree, but there are a few ways to get a cleaner burn, according to the National Candle Association. Avoid buying candles with wire core wicks, since they're more apt to increase soot output than those with cotton or paper wicks. It's also a good idea to keep candles out of drafts, to trim their wicks before burning and to extinguish them with a candlesnuffer rather than blowing them out. I once had a client who loved candles, yet as an asthmatic, was highly sensitive to smoke. She discovered she could burn clusters of candles in the fireplace, where emissions go up the chimney, not her nose.

6. **Litter boxes:** Kitty may like a warm, air-dried bottom, but keep her toilet away from a heating or air-conditioning vent unless you want the granules and the you-know-what to hit the fan.

DUSTING FOR MUMMY

Dust removal can go too far, as was the case at the Baroda Museum in India, where an overzealous janitor opened an airtight display case and gave the mummy inside a good vacuuming. In the process, he loosened the 3,000-year-old bandages, mangled the nose and sucked the paint off two toes. The curator in charge, according to the Associated Press, is now directing operations at another museum.

Quicker Picker Uppers

We don't have to be slaves to dust busting with these common and not so common tools and techniques:

- ✿ **A clothes dryer:** Curtains get dusty fast, but unless they're dirty, simply toss them in the dryer and turn on the fluff cycle for about five minutes.

- ✿ **Laundry starch:** Spray curtains with the stuff, and dust won't have a chance to stick.

> "Your house doesn't pass the white glove test? Luckily, no one wears gloves anymore."
> —Mary McHugh, *Family Circle* magazine

- ✿ **An automatic dishwasher:** Instead of dusting a mass of porcelain or glass knickknacks, position them carefully on the upper rack of the dishwasher and let the delicate cycle do the dirty work for you.

- ✿ **A rubber-lipped dustpan:** Rubber bends over backward to accommodate even the finest dust.

❀ **Lint-free dust cloths:** Electrostatic cloths are not only lintless, they're super-absorbent, long lasting and chemical-free. Toss them in the wash, but leave out the bleach and fabric softener, since both can cut a cloth's absorbency.

❀ **A slightly dampened dry mop:** A dry mop makes dust fly. A little water makes it stick.

❀ **A sock-on-a-stick:** Rout out dust bunnies under the fridge by rubber-banding a slightly dampened thick cotton sock to the end of a yardstick. Better yet, get a pliable child to do the deed.

> "Our house has gone past the 'lived in' look. It has more of a 'no survivors' look. There are no bugs. The dust has choked them to death."
>
> —Phyllis Diller,
> *Housekeeping Hints*

THE DUSTY FACTS OF LIFE

- Seventy-five percent of a home's dust consists of shed skin cells.
- The EPA claims the air inside our homes is so polluted, it's among the top five environmental threats to our health.
- A smoker's home has twice the amount of dust as a normal home.
- Dust-laden air ducts reduce the efficiency of a heating and cooling system by as much as 50 percent.

DESIGN FOR LIVING

A Dust Deflecting Headboard

Wood and metal headboards can get pretty dusty with all those linen changes, blanket shakings and pillow fights. And they're not the most comfy props for reading in bed. A fabric covered, padded headboard, however, is both comfortable and dust-free (at least it *looks* dust-free). It's also a cinch to make.

Simply have the lumberyard cut a sheet of half-inch-thick plywood in a semicircle or rectangle so it's the same width as the head of the mattress. Place the board on a sheet of polyester batting, and cut the batting about three inches bigger all around than the board. Attach the batting to the back of the board with a staple gun. Place the batting-covered board on the wrong side of comforter-coordinating fabric (the companion sheet works well) that's cut about four inches larger than the board. Staple the fabric to the back as well, stretching it so it's a tight fit.

Attach the headboard to the wall with L-brackets, positioning its bottom so it's a few inches lower than the top of the mattress.

Sweet dreams.

(**Note:** A quilt or quilted fabric works even better, since you can skip the batting. Just make sure it's not too thick to staple.)

LIFE MATTERS:

Dust in the Wind

Dust will always be with us, but the opportunity to play with a child, lunch with a friend or walk in the woods on a beautiful day may not. Never let the pursuit of dust and dirt take precedence over life's more rewarding pastimes.

Part III

Whether or not extra hands lighten the load,
we need to give up the crippling
pursuit of perfection.
Nature rejoices in imperfection.
We can too.

L
I
F
E

Forget Perfection

CHAPTER ELEVEN

The Kama Sutra of Cleaning

*"The great question I have not
been able to answer is:
What does a woman want?"*

—Sigmund Freud

Swept Away: The Ultimate-Aphrodisiac

Even after eight months of unemployment, a weight gain of 35 pounds and a hair loss of major proportions, David Delvechio is still irresistible to his wife, Julie. Is it because he indulges her with baubles and whispers sweet nothings in her ear? "Not really," said Julie with a laugh. "One of the main reasons I'm still hot for him is because he's considerate enough to share the chores. When I grill the fish, he tosses the salad. When I wash the car, he vacuums it. When the dishwasher needs emptying, I don't need to ask, he just does it," she said. "We're a true team, and I love him for it."

"Our marriage is so different from my first, where my husband's only contribution to running things was hiring the kid next door to mow the lawn," continued the hairstylist. "I'd put in a full day in the shop, then come home to cook, clean and help the kids with their homework. I not only felt too tired for romance, I felt resentment," she said. "He thought I was frigid. Maybe I was, but there was a reason. I think he'd be surprised if he knew how sexual I really am."

If men only knew how easy it is to keep their sex lives active, they'd save themselves a lot of time and energy, believes author and psychologist John Gray. In his book *Men Are from Mars, Women Are from Venus,* Gray listed "101 Ways to Score Points with a Woman." Twenty-one of those points involve doing chores, including washing the dishes, making the bed and offering to pick up items at the market on the way home.

"A woman's sexual satisfaction is affected by every aspect of the relationship; for a truly happy relationship, intimacy in the kitchen is as important as intimacy in the bedroom."
—Joyce Brothers, psychologist

"Those little things make a huge impact in a relationship," maintains Gray. "Men focus on the big stuff and don't realize it's the little stuff that makes a difference to a woman. Doing chores is one of the best forms of foreplay."

On the flip side, Gray believes that shirking chores can cool a relationship. "When she feels responsible for everything, her ability to enjoy sex is diminished," he explained. "Women need to relax before they can enjoy lovemaking. Men don't understand this—they use sex as a way to relax. Anything that he can do that says 'I see you, I hear you, I help you' helps her cope with the stress of her day."

The Dirty Truth

Sharing chores seems like an easy path to bedded bliss, yet cleaning incompatibility is right up there with kid and cash conflicts in many households. According to a survey conducted by The Soap and Detergent Association, almost half of all married and cohabitating couples fight about housework. The arguments range from who should do it to how frequently and thoroughly it should be done. Not surprisingly, young newlyweds lock horns on the subject more than their longer married counterparts (59 percent versus 34 percent). Children in the home aggravate the issue. Fifty-five percent of couples with children report they bicker over cleaning, compared with 38 percent of households without kids.

> "Blessed are they who make the bed without asking, for they shall enjoy the fruits of it later."
>
> —Anonymous

Keeping Score on Chores

To add to the problem, both partners see themselves as paragons of cleanliness. According to a Procter & Gamble survey of America's cleaning habits, women say they spend about eight and a half hours a week cleaning, and their mates about two and a half hours. Men, however, insist they put in nearly five hours a week and believe their wives clean only about six hours a week.

But "he says/she says" hardly matters when you both run out of underwear or the floor gets so grubby the baby sticks to it. What does matter is that a couple finds an equally acceptable level of cleanliness and a way to maintain it together. The latter may take some strategy.

ARE YOU GETTING ENOUGH?

How often and how deeply you both clean is a lot like making love. The frequency and technique don't matter as much as the mutual satisfaction with both.

A Dozen Ways to Get What You Want

1. **Ask for it.** Often the reason he doesn't offer help is that he may not notice the dirty dishes in the sink or the laundry spilling out of the hamper. Besides, points out John Gray, there may be cultural differences. "On Mars," he maintains, "it is rude to offer help unless you are first asked."

> "Happy is the household where each does more than his own share."
> —A. W. Ku
> *The Tao of Cleaning*

2. **Stimulate a sense of giving.** Rather than keeping score, the Delvechios try to outdo each other by giving more than expected. Julie hauls out the trash and does minor repairs when she knows David is too tired or busy to do so. And David takes over the bills when Julie's in a pinch. "It's like lovemaking," said Julie. "The more we give, the more pleasure we get in return." John Gray concurs: "We're always happiest when we're giving unconditionally."

> "The best way to avoid dishwashing is to have your partner eating out of your hand."
> —Irish proverb

3. **Butter up your baby.** "Dave is great around the house, but his input is something I've carefully cultivated," admitted Julie. "I'll say something like 'Where do you get the stamina to wash all the windows at once?' Or 'I would never have the strength to move that sofa when I vacuum.'" Flattery may get you everywhere.

4. **Stay positive.** "When you ask, 'Would you pick up your stuff in the bedroom?' and he asks 'Why?' you respond with 'It's so much nicer when it's clean—I really like it,'" suggests John Gray. Gray believes when it comes to dealing with someone who has committed his life to making us happy, we need to encourage that goal, not repress it. "A man needs to feel loved in an accepting way to improve," he contends. We all do.

> "Find a partner with similar levels of tolerance for dirt and messiness—someone who does not avoid work."
>
> —A.W. Ku
> *The Tao of Cleaning*

5. **Capitalize on his prowess.** If he's artistic, sell the creativity factor of certain jobs. Cooking, for instance, can be both creative and relaxing, especially if there's a sous chef (you) on hand. If he's technical, encourage him to research, purchase and test-drive machines, like the vacuum cleaner and the leaf blower. When I didn't have time to shop for a new washing machine, I asked my husband to do it. Being highly methodical, he consulted *Consumer Reports,* then shopped around for the best deal. By the time it was installed, he felt so territorial about it, he started washing his own clothes and has even offered to wash mine. I've decided not to push my luck.

6. **Arouse culinary latency with virile equipment.** L'Equip's Model 228-RPM blender, for instance, has a jetlike tachometer that displays its powerful engine revolutions per minute. Pro Pots makes slow cookers that resemble sport balls. And a George Foreman Grill has been known to turn the most reluctant chef into a barbecue champ.

7. **Go for the big "O" together.** Organizing the garage in tandem, or some other mutually shared space, increases the chances of things being returned where they belong, since you've worked out a system as a team. At least, that's the dream.

8. **Thank Dad.** Encourage the kids not only to help Dad but also to voice their appreciation for all he does—whether it's bringing home the bacon or frying it. Fathers need respect from their families, yet get so little of it. Check out any sitcom, and Dad is almost always the buffoon—not a healthy role model for anyone.

9. **Allow for creativity.** Maybe you don't clean the toilet with cola and an old back brush, the way Dave Delvechio does, but as his wife, Julie, points out, "If it gets the job done, why argue?"

10. **Lavish praise in public.** Next time you're having dinner with other couples, say something like, "I can never make lasagna as well as Jim." Or "Bob is so good with the kids, they always behave for him." Or simply "It was Tom's idea," when something has gone well. "Men are fueled by acknowledgment," stresses John Gray. "They want to take credit for whatever possible. That's why they don't stop and ask directions—because someone else gets credit."

11. **Don't complain.** "Today's woman wants a 1950s 'wife' in her man," claims a male friend, who wants to protect his identity from his wife-wanting wife. "Yet she's going about it all wrong. You can't bitch endlessly about the cooking and the cleaning and expect a guy to want to do it."

> "Guys do not get enough credit for being domestic. This is because the people who give out the credits for being domestic are—not to generalize or anything—women."
>
> —Dave Barry

12. **Be blatant.** Writer Dave Barry reports that one of his readers divulged how she gets her husband to do the laundry. "I tell him it gets me hot," she said. So hot she makes love to him "right by the washing machine." Barry describes this tactic as "unleashing a nuclear device in the housework wars," and asks men, "Are we that weak, that pathetic, that STUPID?" He answers his own question: "Let's remember to hand-wash those delicates."

When Mr. Clean Loves Ms. Mess

Females are supposed to be the neat ones, right? Not according to the housekeeping staff at the Novotel hotel in New York, who report that men are more likely to unpack their luggage, iron and hang their clothes on arrival than women.

That's no surprise to me. As a child, I rarely hung up my clothes, and I could out-slob my five brothers any day of the week. I was grounded so many times for the revolting state of my room, it was the neighborhood joke. It's still a struggle to overcome the mess-maker within, but I've made strides.

Fortunately, the Mr. Clean I married and I have produced one fairly organized offshoot, our oldest daughter, Kelley. Unfortunately, her sister, Lisa, has inherited my long line of disorderly genes and is about to marry Mark, a guy who would rather tidy up than wind down on her laundry-laden sofa.

> "I am in charge of the laundry at our house. I like my work. It gives me a sense of accomplishment. And a feeling of involvement with the rest of the family."
> —Robert Fulghum, *All I Really Need to Know I Learned in Kindergarten*

Will Mark make his mark on the mess? Can love clean up the differences? Time will tell.

When Queen Anne Loves Lazy Boy

Let Go of Clutter author Harriet Schechter is so good at organizing, she went pro years ago, just about the same time she met Henry, the messy man who was to become her husband. Henry, explains Harriet, is easygoing and good-natured, so messiness—his own and anyone else's—doesn't bother him a bit. However, neither wanted feelings of resentment over housework, so they found a way to share the load.

"I created a list of ongoing chores that we divided according to what each was most inclined to do," said Harriet. "It turned out that the things I hate—like taking out the garbage, gardening and car maintenance—

> "Women have to stay behind to pick up the dirty clothes."
> —Opal Pickles (from the comic strip *Pickles*, by Brian Crane) on why women live longer than men

are tasks Henry doesn't mind. And the things he hates—like laundry, cleaning and organizing—don't bother me. The tasks we both avoid—like cooking, washing dishes and errands, we agreed to share or alternate."

Harriet and Henry have been married for eighteen years, perhaps proving if you can work out chores, you can work out anything in a relationship.

"You want a cheerful, long-lasting marriage? Separate bathrooms. And don't ever let your loved one squeeze your toothpaste."
—George Burns, actor and comedian

Scoping Out a Future Helpmate

"Just like how good a guy dances will tell you how good he'll be in bed, you can pretty much tell how good a guy is going to be in the broom closet by the way he keeps his car," claims New York literary agent and standup comedian Janet Rosen. "If the car is full of food wrappers, newspapers and sweaty running gear, you'll be picking up after him for a long, long time."

"Same thing if he's a messy eater," she claims. "Sauce in that manly stubble is a sure sign of errant toothpaste caps and dirty socks on the sofa for years to come."

"It can go the other way, too," she warns. "If he's too picky with the smudges on the white-walled tires or compulsive with the napkin dabbing to the chin, you can bet he'll be alphabetizing your underwear drawer in no time and making love only on 'your' side of the bed."

"Of course, that can be a good thing too," she concedes.

Avian Arousal

According to a study in *Nature* magazine, older female bowerbirds are attracted to males who perform sexually charged mating dances, while younger females prefer males who build the most elaborate bowers. Males comply by adorning their love nests with flowers, fruits and found objects, often blue, since scientists say that's what the female prefers.

Researchers theorize that the younger, less-experienced females are frightened by the intensity of the mating moves and look for less-threatening skills, like decorating.

Female bowerbirds aren't the only fowl that like their surroundings appealing. New Zealand zoologists at Queensland University discovered that the tidiest male sparrows—those that keep the nest free of fleas and ticks—are more attractive to female sparrows than males with less fastidious habits.

The Perils of Procrastination

Chore evasion can have dire consequences in some cases. According to a May 28, 2003, BBC story, a sixty-two-year-old Scottish woman stabbed her forty-seven-year-old domestic partner to death with a kitchen knife because he shirked cleaning. Edinburgh defender Geoffrey Mitchell told the court that the victim, Andrew Brunton, had spent most of the day in bed. When his partner, Kathleen Sherlock, asked him to clean the flat, Brunton replied, "In a minute."

"In a minute" turned out to be too long for Kathleen Sherlock. "She explained she just gave him a 'poke' on the leg with a knife and told him, 'Right, move yourself.'"

"She said it was her intention to move him, but she had just gone too far," said her attorney.

Sherlock later admitted to "prodding" her partner three times with the knife.

Brunton died from catastrophic bleeding from the thigh.

Other Men, Other Cultures

♌ According to a United Nations study, American men put in about half the time their wives do on the kids and chores. In contrast, Japanese men spend about a fifth of the time that their wives do on child care and less than a tenth on housework.

♌ A University of Michigan study found that Swedish men do the most housework in the Western world—about twenty-four hours a week, compared with American men, who average about sixteen hours.

> "Wash a man's clothes and you give him clean underwear for a week. Teach him to wash them and you give him clean underwear for life."
> —Anonymous

♌ Portuguese men do less housework than any of their peers in the European Union. They also have one of the highest divorce rates. Since these newly released are mostly clueless about making a home habitable, they're turning to Vida-On, a Web site that dispenses advice on all things domestic,

> "Men who help with laundry have better sex lives."
> —Peter Post
> *Essential Manners for Men*

from ironing shirts to how often sheets should be changed.

⚖ Cuban law demands that men share housework equally with their wives. How it's enforced one can only imagine. "Señor, I'm giving you a DUI— 'Didn't Undertake Initiative'—for failing to help with the dishes last night."

> "The fantasy of every Australian man is to have two women—one for cooking and one for dusting."
>
> —Maureen Murphy,
> Australian writer

⚖ In Greece on Midwife's Day, or Women's Day, women hang out in the cafés all day while men stay home and do chores. Men, caught outside the house in certain villages of this cradle of civilization, are stripped and drenched with cold water.

DESIGN FOR LIVING

Reaching New Heights in Bed

The floor under the bed is a convenient place to stash bins of extra bedding, out of season clothing, erotica, any number of things. Expand the headroom there with bed risers, cone-shaped gizmos that elevate the bed's legs by as much as six inches. You may need a longer dust ruffle and have to literally leap in and out of bed, but you'll feel like the lofty lady in "The Princess and the Pea."

LIFE MATTERS:

Better than a Therapist?

Some couples find that putting two heads together to find workable ways to keep the household humming is a good way to strengthen the partnership while creating a nurturing nest. Others find that hiring a professional housecleaner, even if it's only on a monthly or even a seasonal basis, is the most workable option.

It may put a dent in the budget, but professional help has been known to be the salvation of many a relationship. It's certainly cheaper and a lot more pleasant than divorce.

CHAPTER TWELVE

Outfitting the Stay-Clean Home

"Prevention is better than cure."

—Erasmus, Dutch scholar

The Wills and the Greys are next-door neighbors who own the exact same three-bedroom floor plan in a twenty-five-year-old development in Oceanside, California. Yet despite each having two kids and the same house-cleaning service, the Greys pay $86 more for a twice-a-month cleaning than the Wills pay. It also takes the crew nearly twice as long to complete the job.

The difference? The decor.

The Greys are avid collectors of everything from Swarovski crystal and Lladro porcelain to scores of silver-framed photos that are displayed on side tables, shelves and counters throughout the home. They've also covered their floors in white marble tiles and pale rugs, draped their windows in billows of fabric and have mounted enough mirror to mimic Versailles.

The Wills have taken a different approach. They recently installed prefinished oak floors throughout much of the house. Windows are hung with simple shades, and sofas and chairs that aren't upholstered

155

in Ultrasuede fabric and leather are slip-covered in chintzes and checks. Collectibles are kept to a minimum, and what is cherished is either kept behind glass or, in the case of family photos, hung on the walls.

> "When you keep your life and the decoration of your house simple, you reduce stress and have more leisure time to enjoy home and family."
>
> —Alexandra Stoddard

It all boils down to a simple truth—how a home is outfitted makes a huge difference in the amount of time and trouble it takes to maintain it.

Furnishing for freedom is hardly a new concept. Back in 1950, home product designers Russell and Mary Wright wrote in their *Guide to Easier Living:* "All over America, we build and furnish our homes, and live in them, as though there were retinues of servants to do the work."

The Wrights advocated practices that are now common—mounting paper towels in the bathroom and attaching lamps on the walls, as well as those yet to catch on—fitting doors on both the front and back of the refrigerator so it can be opened from two rooms and hanging curtains upside down half the year to equalize fading.

The couple believed that cleaning a home should be "fairly pain-less" and maintained that "under certain conditions, it can even be pleasurable."

Cleaning may not be your idea of pleasure, but with the right materials, colors and patterns, it can be a lot less painful.

Four Steps to Cleaning Freedom

1. Furnish for Saturday morning more than for Saturday night. When we outfit a room with the idea that spills, dings and *living* happen, we make it comfortable for all who use it. We also save ourselves the fuss of maintaining what's only meant to impress. "I grew up in a hands-off museum of a house," said Sheri Wills. "So I'm making it a point to keep things livable for all of us."

> "Water rings on the coffee table just show how many great parties you've had."
> —Mary McHugh, writer

2. Consider the maintenance factor when buying anything for the home. White damask upholstery in the living room and shinny copper cookware in the kitchen may look fabulous, but we'll look haggard keeping them that way, or we'll be poorer paying someone else to do it.

3. Learn to love a patina. Once we can see the beauty in timeworn woods, sun-faded fabrics and the imprint of creature comfort on the living room sofa, we're more apt to give up the impossible pursuit of perfection.

4. Cultivate simplicity. When a room is stuffed with stuff, it takes tons of time and trouble to clean it. When it's pared down to what matters—comfortable seating, good lighting and plenty of space to set down a cup or lay out a project—it's both livable and low care.

The Right Stuff

❀ Check out the hot, new, high-performance fabrics now widely available. Just like those silky pants that hold up so well, microfiber upholstery fabrics drape gracefully and resist wrinkles, spots and stains. Crypton, a waterproof polyester that repels germs, mold and even body fluids, is making its way from hospitals to homes, especially those with pets, kids and the incontinent. Sunbrella brand fabric has been a dream come true for patio furnishings because it is fade-proof and sponge-friendly. Now that it has a softer feel and comes in a wide range of colors, it has moved into even the swankiest and sunniest of living rooms.

> "My philosophy of decor is that nothing should be too precious."
>
> —Rachel Ashwell,
> *Shabby Chic*

❀ Choose or create wood finishes with camouflage capabilities. Pickled, distressed and antiqued woods are better at hiding abuse and neglect than fine-grained, dark-stained, high-gloss finishes that show every mote and water ring. Sheri Wills' family room coffee table gets a workout as a fort, arts and crafts center, and snack table. But before it went to work, she gave the unfinished wood a weathered look by rounding the edges with a sander, rubbing them with candle wax and brushing on a coat of diluted paint. She also gave it a few good whacks with a chain, did another light sanding and slapped on a coat of satin-finish polyurethane. "It already looks like it's led an interesting life, so I don't worry about spills and stuff," she said.

❀ Simplify windows. Elaborate window treatments, like jabots, swags and balloon shades are hard-to-clean dirt catchers with their many tucks and folds. Better to hang simple shades or washable curtains in front of dust-sucking windows. Sheri Wills stenciled the borders of her canvas shades in room-coordinating colors and hung simple tab curtains to frame them. The shades are taupe, so dust is nearly undetectable, and the curtains are a crisp, spot-hiding plaid.

❀ Spilled milk? No one will have a cow if you cover kitchen and dining room seat cushions with "vinylized" fabric—a process that adds a spill-proof finish to almost any fabric. Check it out with a design pro or fabric supplier.

❀ Dress a bed with a comforter you can plop on any time of the day. I discovered the hard way that a snow-white comforter doesn't stay that way when there's a serious napper in the house. I know I can always slip it into a washable duvet cover, but I find stuffing a king-sized comforter back into a cover akin to stuffing a sausage. A floral spread now covers our bed.

❀ Replacing the sofa? Buy the new one with loose seat and back cushions so they can be flipped when they're worn or stained. Loose cushions are also more comfortable than a sofa with a tight seat and back.

❀ When it's time to replace a piece of furniture, go for something that sits flat on the floor, since leggier pieces are hard-to-vacuum hideouts for dust bunnies. Many hotel chains, including Sleep Inn, have taken this bolt-to-the-wall, flat-on-the-floor approach with bed frames, nightstands and other cabinetry to discourage theft and to ease maintenance.

❀ Order furniture with casters whenever there's a choice. A good set of wheels makes the heaviest pieces easy to move for conversation and cleaning.

Do More with Less

➷ Master subtraction. The biggest barrier to a stay-clean home is clutter, so a little judicious deleting can pay off big time. Rather than adding another plant or pillow, experiment by removing a few items from a room. It may look a bit spare at first, but the eye adjusts and then welcomes the new space and serenity. Less is often more than enough.

➷ It's a simple law of nature—the more functions a thing has, the fewer things one needs. Investing in double-duty pieces, like the baby potty that flips into a step stool, a trunk that functions as a coffee table or a day bed that works as a sofa, is one way to go. Seeing new possibilities in old possessions is another. With a little fabric and a glass top, a little-used filing cabinet can be turned into a nightstand, and a cut-to-fit cushion can turn a chest into a diaper changing station or a coffee table into an ottoman.

➷ Furnish the kids' rooms in a style compatible to the rest of the home so pieces are interchangeable when the need arises. A bookcase can eventually hold toys in the nursery or trophies in a teen's room. A bureau that once held socks and T-shirts can hold linens and trays in the dining area.

DOUBLE DUTY FOR THE BIRDS

When a burrowing owl decorates its digs, it does so with found scraps of paper, foil and the occasional dead toad, all held together with cow or horse dung.

Why the unusual mortar? Zoologist Douglas J. Levey at the University of Florida explains in *Nature* magazine that using animal poop isn't just a statement of taste, so to speak, it's a way to attract one of the owl's snacks of choice, the dung beetle.

The animal world apparently knows a thing or two about dual-purpose decor.

⚒ Stick to a limited color scheme. There's great flow and flexibility when various tones and shades of just a few colors are used throughout the home. A core scheme of blue and yellow, for example, can be beautifully mixed with green, lavender and peach. A core palette of camel and terra cotta are nicely complemented by gradations of coral, chocolate and ivory.

⚒ Minimize rugs. A rug by a bed or under a table is a cozy, anchoring touch, but a flock of them can complicate cleaning. Bare is not only beautiful, it's a breeze to keep clean.

Go with the Flow

❀ Provide the right backdrop. My friend Julia has always neatly packed away her cosmetics in her bathroom's cabinets and drawers. However, she's married to a guy who not only has more unguents and ointments than she does, he insists on leaving them all out on the counter. It was a bone of contention

between them until they replaced their taupe and white geo-
metric wallpaper with a colorful, free-form floral print. Like
exotic birds in the jungle, all Robert's bottles and jars now
blend with their new surroundings.

❀ Cultivate a taste for printed tablecloths and matching napkins.
Rich florals, plaids and provincial prints are better at hiding
inevitable food and drink stains than their plainer and paler pals.

❀ Pattern and color are usually the way to go with most furnishings and fittings, but there are times when plain white is just
right. White towels and sheets, for instance, can be washed
with chlorine bleach, which is better at stain busting than
color-safe bleach. White sinks are best at disguising soap
scum, toothpaste and hand lotion dribbles, and white toilets
are good at hiding hard-water mineral deposits.

❀ Cracked wall? No matter how often it's spackled and repainted,
Sheri and John Wills have a reappearing and lengthening
crack that runs from the ceiling to the arched window in their
living room. "The house is not only built on fill, it's not
that far from a major earthquake fault," said
Sheri. "When we realized it was a lost cause, I
hauled out my acrylics and turned the crack into
a vine. Every time the wall sprouts a new fissure,
I dab on a few more leaves and tendrils. It'll
probably look like the hanging gardens of Babylon
by the time we move."

"Beauty will
save the world."
—Dostoyevsky

❀ If pets have the run of the place, and most do, consider draping their favorite perches in animal prints to camouflage the
inevitable hair. Julia and Robert have a leopard print bed for

 their Great Dane, Sadie, and the Wills' Dalmatian, Spot, blends right into the zebra print blanket that covers his chair of choice.

🍀 All flooring gets spotted eventually, but flecked and patterned carpeting in a mid to dark tone will disguise more sins than a lighter one. We recently covered the stairs to our garage/basement with low-nap nylon carpeting in a charcoal and camel plaid that attractively hides more dirt than I want to even think about.

> "A home's wrinkles and imperfections may reveal a richer life."
>
> —Phyllis Theroux, writer

More Guerilla Decorating Tactics

⚰ Make a luxurious-looking dust-bunny barrier by double-skirting a bed. In her *Liz at Home* booklet, Liz Claiborne suggests layering two coordinating bed skirts for a custom look. Make the first layer with the bed skirt you want closest to the floor (the darker or printed one would be the most practical choice). Shorten the second bed skirt by lifting the under-mattress section of the bed skirt to six inches and securing it with safety pins every eight to twelve inches around the bed. Liz, by the way, doesn't mention the dust-bunny bonus, but the double skirt not only discourages them from breeding, it better hides those that do.

⚰ Glass-fronted cabinets? If it's a challenge to keep their contents tidy, create a sense of mystery by hanging curtains from rods mounted on the inside of the cabinet doors.

⚥ Avoid getting carried away with a display of objects on a bookcase. Books are better at disguising dust and easier to keep clean than an abundance of silver, glass and ceramic trinkets.

⚥ Pull books toward the front edge of a shelf so there's no visible room for dust to settle. Use the space behind them as a hideout for jewels or that personal stash of chocolate.

⚥ Layer tablecloths. Grandma's treasured lace cloth may have a few gravy stains in the middle, but if it has a shorter one strategically placed over it, who's to know? If it's in good condition, place a larger cloth under it and cover it with a cut-to-fit piece of glass. A square cloth over a long round one has a particularly graceful look on a circular table.

Four Ways to Deal with Sins

1. Strategically place a few decorative pillows and a throw on a sofa to hide stains and other transgressions. Just avoid placing so many pillows that there's little room to sit.

2. Play with your crayons. Crayons and markers can be magic wands on damaged wood. Pros use them to camouflage scratches and even gouges on furnishings, doors, paneling, chair rails and base-boards. With the wide variety of colors available, it's easy to find the perfect match.

"If women only have one head why do they need so many pillows? Am I missing something?"

—Keith, age 30,
Glamour magazine

3. Hide the mess of a chronically unmade, clothes-strewn bed with a room divider. *Sunset* magazine showed one for a teen's room that's made from a 52-inch high, 82-inch long bookcase that runs a little longer than the length of the queen-size bed. This mini-wall not only holds books and bedside items, it hides a multitude of debris. Since it's finished on the back and the area between it and the door is clear, the room looks totally tidy from the hallway.

4. Always buy a little extra paint and wallpaper so you can easily make touch-ups and repairs. It's also handy to have a few extra yards of matching or coordinating fabric to toss over a mess when it gets to you.

Damage Control

❀ Keep a few containers of Baby Wipes strategically hidden around the house to quickly clean dribbles and spills from fabrics. They're especially good to stash in a dining room cabinet to rescue good clothes and table linens from dribbles and spills.

❀ Place smooth plastic casters under furniture legs on hard floors to prevent scratches, and spiked ones on carpeting to prevent dents. It's also smart to stick self-adhesive felt pads under floor lamps, recycling bins, wastebaskets and other items that can wound wood.

> "Don't remove all the scars and history from antiques. Restoration is a good thing, but beware the overzealous refinisher."
>
> —Charles Spada, interior designer, *House Beautiful*

✿ Drape a washable cotton throw over a favorite upholstered chair for comfort and protection. I keep one on my recliner's arm to use as a cover when I give myself a manicure, pedicure or just a heavy slather of hand cream. It's also a good blankie.

✿ Dimples are cute on faces but not on counters. Be sure to seal granite and other pitted stone regularly, since those little depressions catch and trap crud.

DESIGN FOR LIVING

Screening Secrets

Screens are versatile devices when we want to hide a messy desk or a cluttered corner. They're so multi-talented—they can direct traffic, create a foyer, make space cozier and add interesting angles to a room.

I used a short one that I fashioned from an appliance carton and adhesive paper (in my Contac paper years) to screen my culinary chaos from the dining room. It also hid a mountain of laundry when I was too tired or, more accurately, too lazy to deal with it.

I made a taller one from three pieces of hinged plywood and leftover wallpaper that blocked drafts when it was cold and hid an ugly radiator when it wasn't.

I've seen screens crafted from old doors, windows and shutters as well as boards covered with everything from government-issue maps to upholstered silk. Folding screens are the best friends of decor: They're there when you need them and disappear when you don't.

LIFE MATTERS:

Flawed and Fabulous

The historic scars in antique furnishings are not only interesting and easier to live with, they can make a valuable piece even more so. When a guest on "Antiques Roadshow" had his newly refinished highboy appraised, he was dismayed to find that had the worn and dinged finish been left intact, the 200-year-old piece would have been worth $120,000. But because it had been stripped of the "rich patina of history" and refinished (beautifully, I might add), it lost more than half its value.

Like fine old furniture, a few flaws and the "patina of life" can make us more interesting and valued to the world.

CHAPTER THIRTEEN

Heavenly Chore Cheaters

"Clean good. Cleaning bad."

—Jerry Seinfeld

The intermingling scents of Clorox and Bounce have always had a soothing effect on Sarah. It reminds her of clean sheets, Mom and apple pie order. She cultivated this scent during her single years in her tiny Greenwich Village apartment. But when she and her new husband, Joe, moved to a Brooklyn fixer-upper, started a mail-order business, and adopted two sons and a puppy, the scents that filled their days were of wet diapers and dry rot.

It wasn't that the couple didn't love their full house and fuller life, they just felt wistful for little things like a clean floor and windows they could actually see out of.

"Besides," Sarah admitted, "being a parent and running a business, I've discovered three truths about life: vacuuming sucks, dusting's a drag and swabbing a toilet is an unspeakable act."

If you too love clean, but hate cleaning, know there are easier, less orthodox ways to outwit the dirty work.

Preventative Measures

⌐ Slip off the shoes. Asians have been doing this for centuries, not only to keep the inner sanctum free from "the dirt of the world" but to maintain quiet and foster a closer connection with the earth. "Besides the obvious sanitation, there's something freeing about going shoeless indoors claims," Joyce Yamada. "It's like changing out of a business suit into a velvet bathrobe."

> "It's hard to be funny when you have to be clean."
> —Mae West

⌐ Keep a pair of garden clogs by the door for runs to the mailbox, the garden or the neighbors. "I encourage everyone in the household to wear easily slipped-off shoes," said Yamada. "When there are no ties, tabs or buckles to deal with, we're more apt to leave the dirt at the door."

⌐ Most dogs don't wear shoes, so keep either a small towel or a container of premoistened wipes by Rover's door. You'll be amazed at the crud that comes off paws— crud that would otherwise be tracked through the house.

⌐ Let the wind do the sweeping by keeping a porch, deck and outdoor steps sealed with enamel or clear, slip-free sealant. Otherwise, raw wood absorbs dirt and eventually sends it inside.

> "If you don't feel happy walking barefoot in a house, then you're never going to feel at ease there."
> —Nigella Lawson, food writer

⚖ Make all surfaces practical with sealers. A clear coat or two of polyurethane with aluminum oxide makes wood floors nearly indestructible, grout sealer makes tile easier to keep clean and concrete seal keeps the dust down in the basement and garage.

⚖ Keep a vacuum cleaner's width between pieces of furniture so you don't have to rearrange things every time you haul out the Hoover.

⚖ Place houseplants in deep plastic or clay pot liners to prevent water-damaged tables and floors. A layer of pebbles in the liner will protect roots from rotting in excess water, and the drain off will increase the nourishing humidity around the plant.

⚖ Protect a wood table from a potentially leaky flower arrangement by keeping a plastic placemat under the tablecloth or table runner, or put the mat directly under the container itself.

Fresh Approaches

❀ Do the "twelve-minute two-step." Once the boys are tucked in, Sarah and Joe set the kitchen timer and quickly tidy up in the one-eighth of an hour they've allotted. "It's amazing what we can do in that short time when we focus," said Sarah. "It's not exactly *House Beautiful*, but the place always looks good enough to kick back in without feeling guilty."

❀ Tune into natural opportunities. Change the bed linens when you both get up on the weekend, clean out the fridge just before marketing, scrub down the shower while it's still a little steamy. Working with natural rhythms makes chores flow.

❀ Reclaim the dumping ground. Joyce Yamada's boys always dumped their junk on the kitchen table after school, until she got in the habit of setting the table for the next meal immediately after clearing the dishes of the last one. "Their stuff ends up in the family room now, but at least we don't have to bulldoze it to eat," she said. "Besides, meal prep seems so much easier when the table's already set."

> "When I was first married, in 1943, I watched young gals spend all their time cleaning as though they were going to entertain. I do the opposite: I entertain, but I don't clean."
>
> —Franny Taft, eighty-three-year-old Cleveland Institute of Art professor, as told to *Real Simple* magazine

❀ Figure a way to sweeten a dreaded chore. I hate doing paperwork, but I've learned how to take the bite out of it by sandwiching it between more pleasant tasks so I don't burn out. I set my timer for twenty-minute paper-plowing sessions and intersperse them with more pleasant tasks, like watering my houseplants, arranging a bowl of branches or flowers and stacking magazines for the evening's perusal.

❀ Focus on cleaning from waist level down. "Most people look down, not up," writes P.J. O'Rourke in *The Bachelor Home Companion: A Practical Guide to Keeping House Like a Pig.* "So they'll notice dust rats on the floor before they spot cobwebs on the ceiling."

> "Show me a household with a dog in it and I'll show you a household with numerous low-altitude wall stains."
>
> —Dave Barry

Cool Tools

⚘ The outside of the house may look like it needs a paint job, but it might just need a good shower. Buy or rent a high-pressure hose that blasts away dust, soot and other debris that dulls and deteriorates an exterior.

⚘ Don't do windows? You might be tempted with a special bottle of exterior window cleaner hooked onto the garden hose. Flick the sprayer to "Rinse" to spray off heavy dirt. Flip to "Clean" to apply the product, and then back to "Rinse." No need to polish—the cleaner has a special sheeting action that dries nearly streak free.

⚘ Invest in professional cleaning equipment like a serious squeegee and hefty sponges. I recently found a telescoping handle at a janitorial supply shop. Attached to a broom or mop, it clears away sky-high dust and cobwebs like a mega magic wand.

⚘ Find a cleaner that works well on most surfaces to save time, trouble and storage space. I like a multiuse product called Simple Green. Depending on how it's diluted, it can clean everything from carpet stains and window screens to cruddy crown molding. I became a believer when I tried to scrub blackened fireplace brick years ago. Nothing worked until I sponged on some of this stuff. The soot vanished, and the brick is now beautiful.

> "There is a Cinderella aspect to my life. But I've swept a lot of cinders too."
>
> —Catherine Zeta-Jones

⅄ Consider a hand-held, cordless vacuum cleaner. This small wonder is convenient for cleaning hard-to-reach, chronically dirty spots—from a sandy car trunk to a hairy bathtub.

⅄ Use vacuum cleaner attachments for heavy concentrations of dust. Window wells, screens and ceiling fans tend to collect more dust than most rags and mops can handle.

⅄ Buy an angle-bristled broom. It's designed for digging into dirt-collecting corners. Choose one with synthetic bristles, since it's more flexible and less apt to shed than straw. It's also thick and pliant enough to tackle fine debris like spilled flour. Hang it off the floor to keep its dust-busting edge.

⅄ Consider a wide, corn-bristled broom for a deck, porch or patio. Its coarser bristles dig chunks of gunk out of cracks and crevices. Make sure to store it inside, since rain will ruin it.

> "My idea of housework is to sweep the room with a glance."
>
> —Slogan seen on an embroidered pillow

HISTORICAL DIRT

Witches and Their Brooms

That humble broom hiding in the back of the closet has led a colorful past. Its brush was originally made of straw from the broom plant, a shrub believed to hold such mystical properties that ancient herbalists prescribed its essence as an aphrodisiac.

Unfortunately, those herbalists, who were mostly women, were accused of witchcraft when the plague hit Europe, so the broom took on a sinister significance.

Up to then, witches were believed to fly through the heavens on chariots, animals and even shovels. But when a coven of witches was reportedly seen performing a ritual dance with brooms, the two were forever linked.

There was such a strong tie between brooms and witchcraft that, according to *The Dictionary of Superstitions,* "A broom accidentally left out on a Saturday night is likely to disappear on its own accord, accompanying other brooms to Sabbath covens, whether a witch needs it or not."

Strangely, a broom is thought to ward off witches in some cultures. Lay it across a doorway, it is said, and a witch will never cross it. Other sweeping superstitions: never bring an old broom into a new house, always sweep in the direction of the floorboards to be lucky in love, never sweep dirt out the door or you'll sweep out your luck and never sweep with a broom between April and June.

As an old English ditty warns:

If you sweep the house with a broom in May
You'll sweep the head of the house away.

Brighten the Bathroom

❀ Forget the mop. Clean and dry a bath- or shower-splattered floor by foot-swishing a washer-bound terry bathmat or towel.

❀ Love long, hot soaks? Use the bath water as a tub cleaner by running the washcloth or back-brush along the waterline as the water drains. Finish off with a few swipes of the cloth or brush on the tub floor.

❀ Replace soap bars, which are made from surface-gunking fat, with liquid cleansers at all sinks and in the tub and shower.

❀ Who needs fancy drawer liners? Line cosmetic drawers with plain white paper towels. Toiletries will not only be easy to find on the white background, spills can be wiped out with the dampened towel when it's time for a change.

> "If God meant us to clean, we would have mops instead of feet."
>
> —Mary McHugh, writer
> *Family Circle* magazine

Cook Up a Cleaner Kitchen

✄ Trim the fat from roasts to avoid splattered grease and airborne smoke. Your oven will thank you, your kitchen surfaces will thank you and your waistline will thank you too.

✄ Be wary of roasting. Cooking with super high heat usually leaves a super sludge of grease in the oven and on its racks.

✄ Flip on the stove fan when you fry, boil or bubble, and save a bushel of time, toil and trouble.

✄ Dice and freeze the veggies you use the most. I make a lot of stir-fried dishes and spaghetti sauce, so my freezer shelves are stocked with plastic snack bags of chopped onions, red peppers and zucchini, as well as shelled edamame beans and bean sprouts. Having favorite ingredients ready to roll is not only a huge time saver, it keeps your countertops and floors free of debris and makes cleaning a snap.

⚱ Spooning is nice for lovers, but don't let utensils and bowls "spoon" in the dishwasher or they won't come clean.

Clean While You Dream

❀ If the water supply is hard and the dishwasher used only occasionally, pour a cup of distilled vinegar onto its floor to dissolve hose-clogging mineral deposits. Let it marinate overnight and run the empty machine through its normal cycle before breakfast.

"Don't turn housework into a job. The benefit package is lousy."

—P.J. O'Rourke, satirist

❀ Constipated pipe? Before calling the plumber, try pouring in a "laxative" of a half cup of salt mixed with a half cup of baking soda followed by a boiling water chaser. Hit the sack, and then flush things out with the full force of the faucet in the morning.

❀ Mix up a quarter cup of white vinegar with a quarter cup of baking soda. Dump it in a toilet that's not apt to be used in the night. Swish it around with a brush and let sit. Flush in the morning. The baking soda will add sparkle while the vinegar will dissolve mineral buildup.

❀ Clean a lightly encrusted, cold oven by pouring a half cup of ammonia into a two-cup measure and placing it in the oven. Let the fumes soften hardened splatters and spills overnight. Add about a cup of water to the ammonia in the morning, wring out a sponge in the mixture and mop up the residue. Who needs caffeine after a jolt of ammonia?

❀ Lay a slightly wrinkled tablecloth over a pad-covered table the night before a dinner party. Mist the cloth with a fine spray of warm water, turn out the lights, and let time and gravity smooth out the creases.

❀ Tumble just-washed curtains in the dryer with a fresh fabric softener sheet and a thick towel. Thread them through their rods while they're still damp. Gravity will pull out most wrinkles by daybreak.

❀ Whites looking a little gray? Clear the fog by soaking them in a slightly concentrated and fully agitated mix of detergent, bleach and laundry booster. Sleep tight, and hit the "wash" button in the morning.

❀ Add about a cap of chlorine bleach to a clear glass vase of water to break down rotted foliage and flower stains overnight. Give it a wakeup shake, rinse until clear and dry with a linen dishtowel.

❀ Sprinkle baking soda on musty carpeting and vacuum the next day. Soda absorbs yucky smells while we snooze.

TRY A DIFFERENT PERSPECTIVE

I hate scrubbing and swabbing, so I do all I can to outwit them whenever I can. But I try to view the rest—clutter control, tidying, pillow fluffing and general sprucing up—more as "home improvement acts" than housework. They are, after all, transformative ways to add order, comfort and beauty to life.

Small Investments, Pretty Big Payoffs

- Install a handheld shower in the bathtub or shower stall. It directs a jet of water to the intended target, be it a child, a Chihuahua or a sudsy shower door. Price Pfister also makes a flexible hose that pulls out of a bathroom sink faucet—just the thing for quickly whisking away whiskers and toothpaste.

- Spray table linens and upholstery with a fabric protector like Scotchgard. Just make sure the cloth is squeaky clean or stains may be set for life.

- Dump the ancient wire-cored toilet brush. The metal can scratch the porcelain, making it more porous and susceptible to stains.

- Stash a box of disposable gloves under the bathroom and kitchen sinks for extra yucky jobs.

- Speaking of yucky, designate different color sponges for the kitchen and bathrooms so the table doesn't get cleaned with the same sponge that mysteriously migrated from the toilet.

Four Ways to Complicate Cleaning

1. **Litter work surfaces.** Small appliances, toiletries and other clutter have to be moved to scrub kitchen and bathroom counters. Plus, all that stuff gets splattered or greasy. Store as much as you can behind closed doors or drawers.

2. **Use gobs of product.** Like hair conditioner and pomade, too much of even a good thing is counterproductive. An overabundance of

carpet shampoo leaves dirt-attracting soap film, a surplus of glass cleaner makes windows streaky and a heavy hand with bleach can weaken fabrics. When in doubt, read the manufacturer's suggested dosage.

3. **Hunt for tools.** When we have to look for a sponge, a rag or even a clothes hanger, cleaning up seems hardly worth the effort.

> "Within every procrastinator lies a perfectionist."
>
> —Pilar Guzman and Jennifer Jafarzadeh, writers

4. **Jump the gun.** Tracked-in mud or wet soil from a toppled houseplant can make a mess on the carpet if it's tackled too quickly. Left to dry, however, it can be vacuumed without leaving a stain. Sometimes it pays to procrastinate.

Regional Cleaning Habits

The Bounty (paper towels) Home Care Council Survey of America's Cleaning Habits found that each area of the country has its own cleaning quirks.

Americans in the Northwest

- Clean the windows more than the rest of the country
- Are least likely to use professional cleaning help
- Get most of their cleaning info from radio talk shows
- Focus most on convenience when buying cleaning products
- Are most likely to think their house is cleaner than a friend's house

Americans in the Northeast

- ❀ Dust more frequently than the rest of the country
- ❀ Are most likely to employ professional cleaning help
- ❀ Spend the least time cleaning
- ❀ Get most of their cleaning info from newspapers
- ❀ Are least likely to think their home is cleaner than their parents' home

Americans in the Midwest

- ❀ Clean the garage more often than the rest of the country
- ❀ Get their cleaning info from TV lifestyle shows
- ❀ Are most likely to focus on cost value when buying cleaning items

Americans in the Southwest

- ❀ Clean their kitchen more than the rest of the country
- ❀ Get most of their cleaning info from magazines
- ❀ Are least likely to think their homes are cleaner than their friend's
- ❀ Are most likely to think their homes are cleaner than their parents'

Americans in the Southeast

- ❀ Clean their bathrooms more than the rest of the country

- ❀ Spend the most time cleaning

- ❀ Glean most of their cleaning info from books

- ❀ Focus most on germ fighting when buying cleaning products

- ❀ Are most likely to believe that "No one cleans as well as I do"

"If you are very efficient, you will have a spotless kitchen, but you will never have the time for a real conversation."

—Geoffrey Godbey, Ph.D., professor of leisure studies Penn State University

DESIGN FOR LIVING

A User-Friendly Broom Closet

Make the utility closet a tidy place for supplies to hang out in instead of a jammed cubicle that smacks us with the broom every time we open the door.

A row of spring-loaded clamps will keep mops, brooms, dustpans and brushes in line, a couple of shelves will hold cleaners and a pretty, glazed shopping bag will stash a cache of rags. Some find a coat of glossy white paint on the walls the best option for making it all pristine and bright, but interior designer Clodagh often paints the insides of her celebrity clients' utility closets fire engine red "to spark the energy" of whoever is cleaning.

LIFE MATTERS:

Find a Focus

Determine which space is the most gratifying to keep clean, then focus your efforts there. Whether it's the living room, the bathroom or the master bedroom, make the space sacred to you. Trying to keep all rooms tidy all of the time, especially if there are kids, pets or slobs in the household, can make the caretaker crazy and the inhabitants on edge.

Besides, it's comforting to have one pure and pristine place to escape to when the rest of the house is in shambles.

CHAPTER FOURTEEN

Wash and Wearable Wisdom

"I use Cheer.
I like the idea of a happy wash."

—Robert Fulghum, *All I Really Need to*
Know I Learned in Kindergarten

Long ago and not so far away, doing the wash was a festive occasion. On the first sunny day of spring, women would pile their laundry into reed baskets, lift the baskets onto their heads and make their way to the newly thawed river. There they would scrub their wraps and loincloths with a mixture of animal fat and wood ash, soak stubborn stains in saved urine and pound out ground-in dirt with sticks and stones.

As their bruised but clean clothes dried on the rocks, the group would tell tales, gossip about their men and watch their children splash in the water.

"In the sixteenth century, human urine was still being used, as it had been for centuries. It was a very cheap source of ammonia, and privies sometimes had a special tub set aside purely to collect it."

—Alison Sim, *The Tudor Housewife*

It was an enjoyable break from the winter confines of the cave, but since it took all day and interrupted more important tasks, washday took place no more than once or twice a year.

Today doing the wash is no longer a social occasion. Nor is it a big deal. The trouble is, it is now so easy, it's estimated that the average household washes 7.4 loads, or about 50 pounds, of laundry a week. That's a lot of gathering, sorting, spot cleaning, folding and putting away—time that could be better spent soaking our own skins or maybe sunning them as we hang with friends.

I decided long ago I wanted more time for these and other pursuits, while still maintaining a well-kept wardrobe that doesn't look like it's been beaten by rocks and soaked in you-know-what. If you do too, you might consider a few of the following tips.

Lighten the Load

⌒ Break the hamper habit. As any good butler knows, newly shed clothes often just need a good brushing and airing, unless, of course, they're hopelessly stinky and stained. Brushing releases spots and lint, while airing frees odors and wrinkles.

> "I have just enough time in THIS life to wash and dry all my laundry. I'll put it away next time around."
>
> —Stephanie Piro, Co-creator of comic strip, *Six Chix*

⌒ Sun-wash. Scientists have long known that the sun's heat and ultraviolet rays kill most odor-causing bacteria, but I discovered this by accident at a Mexican health spa. Every morning that I returned from the mountain or meadow hike, I'd peel off the sweaty T-shirt and bra, drape them over a sunny patio chair to launder later and slip into something else. When I'd get back a couple of hours later, the offending clothes were not only dry, they smelled fresh and clean. Solar power won't remove dirt, but it will make stale and sweat-soaked clothes smell like the great outdoors.

- ꝉ Learn to love dark colors and dense prints. Since they're more forgiving than white and pastel things, they can go longer between washes. I pack nothing but black pants and washable, dark, printed tops when I travel to most places, since I'd rather see the sights than watch my clothes agitate in an alien laundromat.

- ꝉ Dress "errand ready" when hanging around the house, so if you slip out for a quart of milk or a jolt of java there's no chance of dirtying two sets of clothes. "I discovered I look and feel better throughout the day when I gave up the 'no-one's-going-to-see-them-anyway' grubbies," admitted one writer friend. "I no longer have to change clothes if I go out or get caught looking ratty at home."

- ꝉ Wear an apron or a long work shirt when cooking or cleaning to keep the clothes below pristine. The best coveralls don't need ironing, and a few stains can enhance the serious chef or domestic deity look. I know an emergency room nurse who does all her cooking in her spare scrubs, since they cover whatever is underneath and are easy to wash. "If they can keep me clean in the E.R., they can keep me clean in the kitchen," she said.

⚮ Stock up on underclothes. Most of us have enough outerwear to get us through a month of Sundays. What drives us to the washer is the lack of underwear, washcloths and socks. Buy enough to get everyone in the household through at least a couple of weeks, should the machine or its operator break down.

⚮ Make every family member over age ten responsible for his or her own laundry. It's an easy job, provided one person isn't saddled with the wel-fare of everyone else's clothes. The day I noticed my kids' laundry consisted mostly of the clean clothes I had recently folded and delivered was the day I quit as head laundress.

> "I especially like it when there's lots of static electricity, and you can hang socks all over your body and they stick there."
>
> —Robert Fulghum, on the joys of doing the laundry

⚮ Post washer and dryer instruc-tions, along with a stain removal chart, just above the washer and dryer. Sally McVeigh does just that in her Martha's Vineyard cottage, where a steady stream of summer visitors are able to run a load of gritty beach towels and soiled T-shirts on their own. "When it comes to food and clothing, most of my guests enjoy the independence," she said. "And I get to enjoy my guests by encouraging it."

HISTORICAL DIRT

Love and the Laundress

The laundress was the sorceress of the manor in centuries past. She'd concoct boiled brews of pigeon and hen dung, lye and oxen gallbladders, and even human urine to eradicate spots and stains.

Since her work produced so much stench and steam, the laundry area was set apart from the house, often near the stables, giving her a measure of privacy and independence few female servants enjoyed. Consequently, trysts between the laundress and the stablemen were legendary.

"As far as sexual segregation was concerned," wrote Mark Girouard in *Life in the English Country House*, "the laundry was the Achilles' heel of the Victorian country house."

Prevent Laundry Problems

❦ Stuffing is for pillows and turkeys, not for washers and dryers. It leaves clothes less than clean and more than a little wrinkled. A good rule of thumb for a top-loading washer is to keep loads below the top row of tub holes. Leave at least a quarter of the space free in a front-loading washer and in the dryer drum.

❦ Bounce with care. While fabric softener sheets and liquids give clothes a soft feel and pleasant scent, they cut the absorbency of diapers, towels and cleaning rags.

❦ Don't expose a swimsuit to the sharks of hot water and harsh detergent. A rinse in cold water is enough to flush out salty or chlorinated water, and a gentle cold-water product like

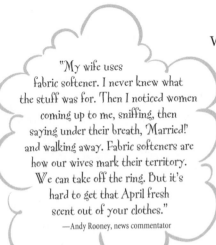

"My wife uses fabric softener. I never knew what the stuff was for. Then I noticed women coming up to me, sniffing, then saying under their breath, 'Married!' and walking away. Fabric softeners are how our wives mark their territory. We can take off the ring. But it's hard to get that April fresh scent out of your clothes."

—Andy Rooney, news commentator

Woolite or Ivory Snow should take care of any sunscreen or ice cream dribbles.

Uncommon Conveniences

The standard clothes-care tools, like an ironing board, sewing machine and portable drying rack, are handy to have in the laundry area. There are also smaller, less conventional gadgets that can make living the clean life a little easier.

- **A tall, wide-mouthed jar:** When there's only a bra and silk panties to wash, pour in water and a little cold-water wash, plop in the items, give the jar a few shakes and rinse. I have a half-gallon, empty artichoke jar that functions as my "mini maytag."

- **A salad spinner:** Drop in a sopping sweater and give it a spin. Surplus water will wick right out. Buy the largest you can find, and wring two sweaters for the price of one.

- **A tennis ball:** Toss it into the dryer with a down-filled jacket or vest. The tumbling ball fluffs up feathers and smoothes out wrinkles. Really. It'll whack a down-filled pillow and comforter back into shape as well.

- **Masking tape:** The bikini wax of the laundry room. Place the garment on the ironing board. Press a strip of tape over the offending spot, and zip it off like a bandage. With any luck, the spot will lift off like spare hair on hot wax.

⌣ **An embroidery hoop:** Clamp the stained section of the washable item within the frame, hold it over the sink and *carefully* pour a boiling teapot of water from a height of about three feet over it. The force and heat of the water should shoot the stain right down the drain.

⌣ **An old toothbrush:** A soft one is best for scrubbing stains off fabric, just as it is for scrubbing plaque off teeth.

⌣ **Cotton swabs:** A tiny dab of chlorine bleach on a spotted white T-shirt (washed out immediately) or a smidgen of well-placed dry-cleaning fluid on a stained suede boot can be more effective and less damaging than a douse with a less-controlled applicator.

⌣ **Mesh lingerie bags:** In addition to protecting delicates in the washer, these zippered wonders are great for keeping wayward socks and gloves paired in the dryer. Designate one bag for each family member, marking each bag with a dot from different colored laundry markers.

⌣ **A bucket:** Use it for washing out visors, baseball caps and other items that bend out of shape in the machine. Even if there's a utility sink, a lightweight bucket with a sturdy handle is handy, since you can move it when you need the sink for other purposes.

The Ten Commandments of Stain Busting

1. Treat a spot pronto. The longer it sits, the more likely it stays.

2. Look where stains like to lurk: on collars, cuffs and the belly zone.

3. Read the garment care label before reaching for any cleaner. I once sloshed a weak solution of bleach and water on a moldy white rayon shirt. I zapped the mold, but killed its host.

4. Test any treatment on an inconspicuous area, like an inside hem or the selvedge edge of a seam. Even plain water can leave its mark on some fabrics.

5. Work from the outside in when treating a stain. Otherwise, it can develop an unholy halo.

6. Keep a stain-removing stick in the kids' rooms and wherever clothes are removed. Betsy Ramberg of Seattle keeps one in the bathroom medicine cabinet, so when her kids soak in the tub, she treats their clothes with the stick. "I find the sooner I treat stains," she said, "the more likely they'll come out in the wash."

7. Blot, don't rub. Rubbing can drive a stain deep into fibers.

8. Since heat can seal a stain for life, use cool water soaks, and remove any spot before machine drying or ironing.

9. When in doubt, consult a professional dry cleaner.

10. If the situation is truly hopeless, cover the stain with an appliqué, or turn it into a design with a bit of embroidery or a colored laundry marker. My kids' playclothes went through early childhood under a colorful assortment of bugs, butterflies and flowers, which, for a time at least, the kids thought were cool.

TAKE A BITE OUT OF GRIME

Today, we have an arsenal of chemical solvents to rout out the toughest stains, but science may be taking us back to more natural potions. Researchers at Whittier College in California recently found that an enzyme in venom extracted from the deadly Florida cottonmouth snake (aka the water moccasin) removes bloodstains from denim better than commercial products do.

Keep Your True Colors

❀ Turn colored clothes inside out before they go into the washer and dryer. In a test conducted by *Real Simple* magazine, jeans that were washed and dried ten times this way were "significantly less faded than those dried right side out." All fabrics are also less likely to abrade and pill when washed and dried this way.

❀ In addition to separating whites from colors, keep the super grungy away from the lightly soiled—sloughed-off dirt can turn neighboring items dingy.

❀ Cool off. Hot water (120°–130°) is good for maintaining whiteness and for cleaning grubby clothes, but it can also fade colors faster than a warm (90°–110°) water wash. The cooler the water, the truer the color.

❀ Hang in the shade. Drying a colored garment out of direct sunlight will preserve its dye better than drying it in the sun.

❀ Always launder or dry clean all pieces of a dyed-to-match outfit so items fade together. I once had a periwinkle blue warm-up that was practically my daily uniform. Trouble is, I washed the pants more than twice the times I washed the jacket, and it eventually looked it.

❀ Avoid spots and streaks on fabrics by agitating detergent and additives in the wash water before dumping in clothes.

❀ Things looking a little gray? White soaks—a quarter cup lemon juice or hydrogen peroxide diluted in a gallon of water—are effective at safely brightening T-shirts and other white cottons without weakening fabric the way chlorine bleach can. Or give them new life in a hot black tea solution (Lipton is good). Depending on the fabric, tea strength and the length of the soak, the finished color will range anywhere from warm ivory to deep caramel.

Lessen Lint

⚘ Towels, blankets and rugs love to share fuzz in the washer and dryer, especially when there are dark knits, cords and other softies rubbing against them—so keep them apart.

✑ Check all pockets before washing. Many a small tissue has left its woolly mark on a dark load.

✑ Clean the dryer's lint filter before starting each new load. A full filter can't catch lint, but it can catch fire. In fact, some folks use dryer-trap lint as fireplace kindling.

Avoid Pilling, Snags and Other Wardrobe Abuses

❀ Button buttons, zip zippers, snap snaps. Open closures are known to have their way with fine fabrics.

❀ Keep rough guys, like denim, away from softies, like silky knits, in both the washer and dryer.

❀ Don't overdry anything. High heat fries fabric and frays hems.

ONE WAY TO TREAT THE WASHDAY BLUES

A washing machine is traditionally the most trouble-free appliance in the house, but when it goes bad, it can make some people very, very mad. As was the case when a thirty-seven-year-old Chippewa Falls, Wisconsin, man got so angry with his washer, he pushed it down a flight of stairs, shoved it onto his driveway and shot it with a gun.

Outwit Ironing

⅄ Weigh a wardrobe with fabrics that don't have pressing needs. Knits, denim, wool, nylon, flannel, fleece, permanent press cotton, seersucker, Microfiber and Lycra keep a wardrobe working, while wrinklers, like pure linen, raw silk and untreated broadcloth cotton, tend to languish in an ironing basket.

> "You can't get spoiled if you do your own ironing."
> —Meryl Streep

⅄ Set the dryer on permanent press for most fabrics, since it ends with a wrinkle-blasting cool down.

⅄ Release creases and prevent twisting by giving each item a good snap as it comes out of the washer. Ditto for the dryer.

⅄ Catch a wrinkle in time by hanging barely damp clothes still warm from the dryer. I find that even clothes that do need ironing are better hung than folded, since they're apt to shed wrinkles in a day or two. They're also easier to keep track of than those stuffed in an ironing basket.

⅄ If you're lucky enough to have an outdoor clothesline, hang out wash on a windy day, since a breeze billows out wrinkles.

⅄ Leave the bulky travel iron at home. As a former flight attendant, I learned to rid clothes of wrinkles by hanging them in a steamy bathroom on arrival and letting them dry, preferably overnight. If there are any stubborn creases left, I dampen them with a few squirts from a spray bottle or dabs from a wet washcloth and then blast them with a hairdryer while pulling the fabric taut.

⚲ Make ironing something to look forward to by saving it for a favorite TV show or book on tape. Or use the repetitive act as a quiet contemplation. In a *Family Circle* interview, actress, author and producer Marilyn Kentz confided that ironing is therapeutic for her. "It takes out the creases of my anxiety by giving me a sense of completion," said the former *The Mommies* and *Caryl and Marilyn* star. "It becomes a relaxing part of the day."

Shipshape Shoes

❀ Shoes get dusty, scuffed and jumbled on a closet floor and are best elevated in a hanging shoe bag or rack. I once solved my shoe storage problem with a long, low bookcase I found on the sidewalk outside my Boston apartment. I hauled the thing up three flights of stairs and pushed it into my closet, where it neatly (more or less) held my slippers, sandals and stilettos—at least, when I remembered to put them there.

> "Unpolished shoes are the end of civilization."
> —Diana Vreeland, fashion editor

❀ Keep seasonal shoes and boots shapely in storage by shoving cedar shoetrees in them just before they're packed away. "Shoe trees are like Botox for leather," declared Carson Kressley on "Queer Eye for the Straight Guy."

❀ Rotate footwear. We all need a break now and then, and shoes bounce back best with a twenty-four-hour time-out.

❀ Pamper that skin. Like a professional facial, a good cream leather conditioner followed

by a brisk buffing softens leather, protects it from the elements and minimizes blemishes.

❧ Worn heels not only look scruffy, they throw off posture and can ultimately stress the back, knees and feet. Take them to a cobbler at the first sign of wear.

> "A well-designed purse, like a good Louis XV desk, it should have a multitude of secret compartments."
>
> —Amy Fine Collins,
> *Handbags: A Peek Inside a Woman's Most Trusted Accessory*

❧ An artist's gum eraser makes a dandy scuff buffer for suede. Or try the fine side of an emery board for deeper dings. Disguise scratches on dark brown or black leather with a matching laundry marker.

❧ Scuffed beyond the pale? Have a shoe repair shop dye a cute but scratched pair of shoes black.

THE FANTASY PURSE

The perfect purse is not only fashionable and goes with everything, it's also big enough to hold essentials yet small and light enough to prevent back strain. It's designed with just enough compartments to file all that's needed yet not so many to misplace them. It also has some type of closer so a pickpocket can't pick it and an accidental drop can't dump it. In short, it's a well-designed, multidrawed desk, only smaller.

I've yet to find this wonder, but if I do, it will also have:

- Three built-in slots to separately hold cell phone, sunglasses and reading glasses
- A seat belt-type warning system that beeps when a wallet or another crucial item isn't replaced within a preprogrammed time

- A close-to-the-body silhouette, so I don't look like I have more paunches than I already do. It would also be nice not to whack surrounding people and objects.

- The ability to expand to accommodate a book, a bagel or a bottle of water.

- A built-in mirror on the inside flap to discreetly check lipstick on the teeth and spinach between them.

- A contrasting lining so I can quickly spot my wallet.

- An automatic cleaning system that whisks away gum wrappers, about-to-leak pens and mysterious bits of flotsam and jetsam.

DESIGN FOR LIVING

Cheer a Dreary Space

More often than not, the laundry area is a dismal, poorly lit place stuck in a corner of the basement or the back of the garage. Brighten the spot by painting the walls a yummy color, like butter yellow or ripe peach. Hang a cheerful poster of a sunlit scene and add a floor lamp—or better yet a wall-mounted lamp or two—to better spot stains, match socks and read minuscule fabric care labels.

LIFE MATTERS:

It All Comes Out in the Wash

Doing the laundry can be a metaphor for dealing with those nagging little worries we all carry around in our heads. We examine each item, give it the attention it needs, toss it into the mix, walk away from it and put our minds elsewhere. We return to it later, give it a little air and a good tumble, and have faith that things will work out. By the time we assess it again, it has cleaned itself off, smoothed itself out and set the mind free.

Worry? What worry?

CHAPTER FIFTEEN

Life Skills for Kids

"Chores are the making of a child."

—Marguerite Kelly,
family advice columnist

When it came to chores, my five brothers and I could outmaneuver, outwit and outplay our parents any day of the week. Oh sure, we were grounded lots, but we could get around that. My busted brother Larry would slip out of his room onto the porch roof and shinny down the support column out into the neighborhood. Me? I'd simply dream up reasons to be set free: a babysitting job, library research, a church event. No ruse was beneath me.

I feel bad about it today, since my mother was overburdened and underappreciated. Besides, my wily ways came back to bite me when it took years to learn the finer points of home care.

I was determined that my kids would learn what I didn't, but they had the excuses of school sports and homework, which, unlike me, they actually did. Still, I did my best to make sure they did their share around the house—if there's one thing I've learned, chores teach lifelong skills, like respect, responsibility and independence.

Want to cultivate those qualities in your kids, as well as lighten your own load? Try the following tips.

> "Even when freshly washed and relieved of all obvious confections, children tend to be sticky."
>
> —Fran Lebowitz, writer

Start with Their Stuff

Managing their own things is a huge challenge for most kids today because they have so many of them. But there are easy approaches.

- **Limit toys.** It's common sense—the more a person has, the harder it is to keep it all tidy, especially if that person is a child. Yet the average kid is overwhelmed by a ton of toys. Family psychologist John Rosemond believes that a young child should have no more than ten playthings—and only those that are "selected for their creative value." Rosemond is partial to classic toys that stimulate the imagination, such as Legos, Lincoln Logs, TinkerToys, Erector sets and simple dolls, trucks and cars. He also suggests keeping a "toy library," where a child has access to no more than five items at a time—a concept that even the youngest library user can grasp. "I've been preaching this 'less is more' toy philosophy for most of my professional life," said Rosemond. "Those parents who have adopted it have never failed to praise the results."

- **Evaluate possessions together on a regular basis.** This serves a number of purposes, including scaling down to a manageable level of stuff and the opportunity to spend time together doing so. Research shows the more parent time a kid gets, the less dependent he or she is on "things."

🔖 **Have them pay for disarray.** When nursery school teacher Linda Nelson's two teens were toddlers, it was understood that they had to put their toys away after they were done playing with them. Otherwise, Linda and her husband would stash the playthings elsewhere for an extended time. "We always held firm," she said. "The kids wanted those toys available to them, so it was a great motivator to keep them picked up."

Make Them Masters of Their Universe

🌸 **Make it easy.** Install or designate low shelves and cubbyholes in play areas so that toys are easy to grab and put away. "When my kids have a specific, easy-to-reach home for an item, it's more likely to get put back," notes Haley Mullin, mother of five-year-old Chase and nine-year-old Morgan. "We have an imaginary station bin where all the train stuff goes and an imaginary hanger bin where all the airplanes go." The same principle works with food, clothing and every other high-use items. Easy in, easy out.

> "Kids rise to the level you expect."
>
> —Carol Doughty, nursery school director

🌸 **Be colorful.** Different-colored knobs on a bureau are reminders of where clothes belong. One family I know uses a purple knob for pajamas, a tan one for T-shirts, silver for socks and so on. Decals and decoupaged pictures of what should be where are also known to keep underwear from hanging out with outerwear.

❀ **Install lots of fat, reachable hooks wherever clothes tend to land.** I found with my own kids that clothes were more apt to be hitched on a wall than they were hung on a hanger.

NEAT TRICK

Create a Toy Island by defining a play area on the floor with a bedspread or blanket so ongoing projects like puzzles and Lego cities can be confined to one spot yet easily moved without destruction.

Inspire

⌣ Haley Mullin loves watching decorating shows on HGTV, and lately her nine-year-old daughter, Morgan, has taken to watching them with her. "She'll say, 'Hey that's really neat!' or 'Mom, I know what we can do in my room,'" said the Redondo Beach, California mom. Mother and daughter recently saw a simple idea for a canopy above Morgan's bed. Haley installed a couple of drapery rods in the ceiling and hung curtains from above the head and foot of Morgan's bed. "Morgan loves her new bed," said Haley. "And she knows if her room is messy, it's not going to look pretty."

⌣ Point out the perks of organized possessions. Things look cool lined up and stacked and are less apt to be lost. Also, because there's less wasted time spent looking, there's more fun time spent playing.

⚖ Keep score. Joan Rubin, a Rancho Santa Fe, California, mother of three now-grown kids kept a chore chart posted on the fridge for years. It's a system she swears by, since it encourages both responsibility and kindness. "Every little act was worth a certain amount of change, so if you were fabulous and made your bed, were ready for school, were kind to your brother and sister, and did good deeds that went above and beyond, you could make pretty good money in a week," she said. "If you slacked off, you could lose money. So instead of nagging, I'd say something like 'I'm thinking about the cha-a-a-r-r-r-t,' and they'd get to it. They liked the assessment. Best of all, they were able to evaluate themselves on a daily basis, which spilled over into other areas of their lives like schoolwork. A chart takes dedication, but anything that works does."

"Everybody knows how to raise children, except the people who have them."
—P.J. O'Rourke, *The Bachelor Home Companion: A Practical Guide to Keeping House Like a Pig*

A GOOD DEAL

Professional organizer Julie Morgenstern used to charge her now-grown daughter two dollars every time she left the house a mess. "I called it my maid's fee," wrote Julie in *Organizing from the Inside Out*. "My daughter called it highway robbery. Whatever it was, it worked."

Furnish for Tidiness

❀ Place the bed so there's at least two feet of space around it for easier making. I once had a client who waged a constant struggle with her son to make his bed every morning. When I pointed out that even a neat freak would have trouble making a bed that's pushed tight against a wall, she gave it space by pulling it out from the wall and positioning it at an angle. There are still lumps, bumps and floor-sweeping sheets, but the comforter now at least covers whatever is underneath.

❀ Hide a folding card table under the bed or behind a bookcase so there's always a handy surface to spread out a messy project. One mom I know had the legs of a card table shortened to better accommodate her little ones.

❀ Never furnish a kid's room with anything that can't be abused or scrubbed. My friend Sally covered her daughter Meagan's bed with a quilt her grandmother had pieced together from family clothes worn during the 1940s. Even though the quilt was a precious family heirloom, Sally wanted Meagan to "feel" her great-grandmother's love. It was a near tragedy when Meagan left a slow leaking marker in the middle of the quilt. When it comes to furnishing for kids, and everyone else for that matter, life is too short to fuss with the fragile.

> "If your child draws pictures of cows on your woodwork with a felt-tipped marker, you can scrub them with a mixture of one part baking soda, one part lemon juice and one part ammonia, but they still won't come off."
>
> —Dave Barry

DESIGN FOR LIVING

Chalk It Up to Creativity

"Decorating" the walls with crayons and markers seems to be a rite of passage for every child. Rather than continually scrubbing them, go with the flow by covering the lower third of a bedroom wall with chalkboard paint, a special-effects pigment made by Benjamin Moore that turns any wall into a chalkboard. Top it with a strip of glossy (read: washable) molding for a finished look and for a handy place to prop the chalk.

Start 'Em Young, Make It Fun

"It's important to start chores early and believe children can do things," advises Village Church Nursery School director Carol Doughty of Rancho Santa Fe, California. "If you don't, you're telling them they're not capable. It's like potty training—a child is interested at first, but if you miss that opportunity, it becomes a control issue of 'you can't make me.'"

Besides starting young, it helps to make chores fun: rinsing the bathtub with a watering can or buffing a just waxed floor with thick cotton socks or, when that gets old, on a flannel-covered bottom.

Here are a few other ways to ease them into it.

⌛ Buy a pint-sized broom and dustpan for a preschooler, and let her graduate to a hand-held, battery-run vacuum cleaner in a few years. After an explanation of safety procedures, even a six-year-old can suck up crumbs from cushions, hair from the dog's bed and, with those lithe little arms, dust bunnies from under the sofa.

⌛ Let a kid custom design an empty plastic spray bottle with stickers to hold a nontoxic blend of a quarter cup white vinegar to a standard quart spray bottle of water. Give it a whimsical name like "sparkle stuff" or "muck buster," then show how to spritz and rub away spots on the counters, faucets and hard floors. Magic!

⌛ Train a homegrown chef by unearthing simple family recipes and perusing a few junior cookbooks from the library. My daughter Kelley was so taken with our cookie-baking sessions, she could crack an egg on the side of a  bowl and hand separate it by the time she was five. Today she can whip up a meal to impress any guest.

⌛ Haul out the manual mower or the snow shovel. Sure the tractor or snow blower is easier for you, but muscle-powered tools are safer for preteens on up and can get those biceps bulging in time for football or swim season. Besides, wouldn't it be fun to create crop circles in the yard and then "erase" them?

Cultivate Autonomy

We may be able to play reveille, dress a kindergartener, pour the cereal, stuff a backpack and comb a snarled head while applying our own eyeliner and talking on the phone, but letting even the youngest child do for herself boosts confidence and responsibility. Besides, a little more independence on their part couldn't hurt that makeup application on ours. Following are a few ways to help it along.

- ❀ Buy a simple-to-set alarm clock for each child so your kids can get themselves up on school mornings.

- ❀ Fold and stash whole outfits together, including socks, for easy, coordinated dressing.

- ❀ Make dressing doable by avoiding kids' clothes with zippers, buttons, buckles, belts and ties—at least until they develop the motor skills to handle them. Till then, stick to wide-neck pullovers, pull-on pants and skirts, and slip-on or Velcro-closed shoes.

- ❀ Use nonbreakable dishes and glassware when table setters and clearers are still learning.

- ❀ Back up a few demonstrations on how to use the washer and dryer with a posted list of simple laundry instructions. Written instructions help prevent white loads from turning pink, dark loads from turning linty and sweaters from turning into doll clothes.

> "If a nine-year-old is clever enough to play video games, he is smart enough to operate the washing machine."
>
> —Marguerite Kelly

❀ Be patient. Linda Nelson's thirteen-year-old son enjoys preparing meals for himself, but it's been a slow process in terms of "this is how you put things away" and "this is how you clean up after you cook." "I find if a child doesn't catch on, it's 'Okay, let's figure out what's going to remind you to wipe up the counter after you're done,'" said the nursery school teacher. "Then we can go from there."

Socialize Chores

Children are social animals, so they're less apt to balk at doing chores if they're playing on the home team. Besides, working one-on-one with a child is the perfect time to discuss the bigger issues of life, like peer pressure, drugs and where Britney Spears shops.

⚘ Cook together. There's no place like a warm, fragrant kitchen for a good talk while learning a new skill. "Cooking seemed like a lot more trouble than it was worth when they were little," admits Joan Rubin. "But now each one of my kids can prepare an entire meal, though they still leave me the dirty pots and pans."

⚘ Go one-on-one with a child washing the dinner dishes. There's something about coming clean in the sink that encourages coming clean in other areas of life.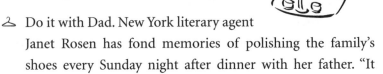

⚘ Do it with Dad. New York literary agent Janet Rosen has fond memories of polishing the family's shoes every Sunday night after dinner with her father. "It wasn't something I thought much about at the time," she admits. "But it was a close, cozy thing, especially since he'd tell me funny stories about his boyhood." A University of California Riverside study of 3,563 children and their parents suggests that school-age children who do chores alongside their fathers have more friends, are happier and behave better in school.

⚘ Invite a child to garden with you. My daughter Lisa loved digging in the dirt, planting seeds and witnessing the miracle of growth. And we both enjoyed the side-by-side quiet time.

⚘ Encourage older children to help their younger siblings with their homework, bed making and basic grooming. Urge younger children to do good turns for their older siblings as well—bringing them a snack when they're studying, giving a back rub, running an errand. Helping one another fosters respect and bonding.

Games Families Play

Who says cleaning is all work and no play? Try the following, then make up your own family work games.

✿ **52 Pickup.** Pop on a favorite tune and challenge everyone to see if a room can be picked up before the music ends.

✿ **Crackerjack.** Hide a few stickers, coins or other small surprises around before asking a child to dust. Tell him he can keep whatever he finds after everything is clean.

- **Want Ad.** Special jobs like waxing the car and painting a fence call for special lures. Advertise it on the family message center, outlining the steps and posting the reward.

- **Job Swap.** Each family member makes a list of his or her chores and then trades them with other family members. Little Joe may want to trade his job as Recycling Captain for Busboy next week. Matt might trade Trash King for playing Animal Handler.

- **Market Scavenger Hunt.** Give each person three specific items to find at the grocery store—a small box of orange Jell-O, two perfect lemons and a big box of Cheerios. Once they've placed them in the cart, give them three more till you reach the checkout.

Psychological Ploys

- Hold weekly brainstorming sessions where family members can swap jobs, air gripes and explore new ways of doing things. Just because cleaning supplies have always been carried in a tote doesn't mean a little red wagon can't work as well.

- Keep an ongoing dinner discussion about how the family can help each other, not only with chores but with everyday problems from schoolwork to peer pressure.

- Make sure everyone is playing on the same team. If a young child sees that both parents and older siblings are doing their part, she is more apt to do hers.

⚯ Never nag. Nagging is only heard by a child as a venting of a parent's frustration. "I try not to say 'do this' or 'do that,'" said Linda Nelson. "My mantra is 'It's your choice,' since my kids know we're serious with the consequences."

⚯ Expect mistakes. "I never demanded perfection," said Joan Rubin. "Nothing squelches a child's desire to do something than you saying the results aren't good enough."

> "A kid will run an errand for you if you ask him at bedtime."
>
> —Red Skelton

⚯ Compliment freely. When a child acts responsibly and does a job well, be sure to respond with something like, "You make me proud," "What a good idea!" or "You really know how to make the old car shine." Just be scrupulously honest when dishing out praise. Children have fine-tuned baloney detectors.

⚯ Never complain about cleaning. Attitudes are contagious.

LIFE MATTERS:

Qualities Kids Gain from Chores

Character: Regular household chores underscore a responsibility to the success of the family. "Good character is like good soup," said the sage. "Both are made at home."

Decisiveness: Learning what to toss, what to keep and how to keep it makes a child more discriminating and sharpens his or her decision-making skills.

Self-esteem: Helping a baby brother eat his peas with a spoon, navigating a grandparent through a new computer program or making a salad for tonight's dinner not only gives a child a sense of belonging, it makes her feel good about herself.

Autonomy: Anyone who knows how to prepare a simple meal, do a load of laundry and keep his possessions organized by the time he leaves home is going to grease his way into adulthood.

Part IV

Since flow is in the wind, the
waves and the starry skies, it makes sense to
encourage and enhance it in our homes.
As our surroundings flow, so do our lives.

L
I
F
E

Enhance Flow

CHAPTER SIXTEEN

Your Astrological Cleaning Style

As much as Beth loves playing house, she's always been organizationally challenged. Projects litter her living room and wrinkled shirts hide out in her dryer. It's not that she doesn't like being clean and tidy, she'd just rather take care of people than possessions.

Her sister Kim is another story. Methodical and meticulous, you could do an appendectomy in her bathroom, find the tools to do so and not worry about the germs—though Kim would worry about the mess.

How can two people from the same parents, identical surroundings and only fourteen months apart be so different? Blame it on the stars. Beth is a dreamy Cancer, who doesn't mind if you slosh your spritzer on the sofa, while Kim is a fastidious Virgo, who will wash, dry and put away your plate of fettuccini before you've finished it.

Can astrology be credited or blamed for our domestic dispositions? I like to think so, since my sign could be a scapegoat for my sometimes slovenly ways.

Here's the dirt on what your sign says about your cleaning, organizing and decorating characteristics and how you can best work with those traits.

Maybe domestic bliss is in the stars.

ARIES
March 25–April 20

Symbol: **THE RAM**

In a Nutshell: Spontaneous. Uncomplicated. Optimistic.

Organizing Skills: The Ram is an analytical problem solver who can view a mess with a cool, calculating eye then tackle it head-on. Cluttered closet? "No problem." Messy desk? "Hey, I can handle it." Hungry mob at the gate? "Let 'em eat cake." Rams have a habit of taking on more projects than they can handle, however, thus life is often littered with the undone.

Cleaning Style: Those born under Aries are enthusiastic cleaners, often coming up with novel ways to deal with dirt, like scrubbing the bathroom sink with shaving cream and clearing sky-high cobwebs with a pool scoop. The Ram is also quick and confident but can be a bit careless—ramming furnishings and running over feet with the vacuum cleaner.

Creating Inner Comfort: Since the Ram's element is fire, deep red walls create all the drama she needs without the clutter of excess trappings. This dynamic sign always feels soothed wherever candles are burning or where peppermint, geranium and sweet pea are growing.

Life Outlook: The chase is more fun than the finish.

Kindred Spirits: Vincent van Gogh, Reese Witherspoon, Celine Dion, Liz Claiborne, Charlie Chaplin, Kate Hudson, Elton John, Norah Jones, Eddie Murphy, Conan O'Brien, J.S. Bach, Matthew Broderick, Sarah Jessica Parker, Mariah Carey, Maya Angelou, Jackie Chan, Russell Crowe, Hugh Hefner, David Letterman.

TAURUS
April 21–May 21

Symbol: **THE BULL**

In a Nutshell: Strong. Steady. Sensual.

Organizing Skills: Bulls have a deep need for order, which is challenging since they're avid collectors of everything from deli containers to dollhouses. They're also slow to start a project, but since they like a steady routine, they get the job done by sneaking up on it with small, well-spaced attacks.

Cleaning Style: The Bull thinks things through carefully. "Let's see, does that blood stain need bleach or peroxide?" "I'll wash the windows when it's cloudy so the glass won't streak." These true homebodies, who like complete control of their environments, are good at maintenance, though they tend to get bogged down by doing everything by the book.

Creating Inner Comfort: A sensualist who's a slave to the pleasures of the flesh, just the thought of Dom Perignon in the cellar and Frette sheets on the bed can make Taurus weak in the knees. The Bull may see red when he's in high gear, but he'll find serenity with soft shades of blue and green and pleasure with arrangements of daisies and lilies.

Life Outlook: When I can't blind with brilliance, I'll baffle with bull.

Kindred Spirits: William Shakespeare, Uma Thurman, Leonardo da Vinci, Michelle Pfeiffer, Tchaikovsky, Audrey Hepburn, Katharine Hepburn, Jack Nicholson, Sigmund Freud, Jerry Seinfeld, Renée Zellweger, Willie Nelson, Jay Leno.

GEMINI
May 22–June 21

Symbol: **THE TWINS**

In a Nutshell: Quick. Amusing. Witty. "If any sign could fly," wrote Gary Goldschneider and Joost Elffers in *The Secret Language of Birthdays,* "this would be the one."

Organizing Skills: The Twins want at least two of everything, so clutter can be a major problem. But since generosity is such a strong trait, those born under this sign often give things away as fast as they acquire them. They also like quick, temporary solutions, such as tossing a scarf over a pile or hanging clothes on hooks "for now," which explains those strange little bumps and puckers all over their clothes. A Gemini is also a nimble juggler of projects, though she tends to leave many undone.

Cleaning: Gemini people suffer from FOMO—Fear Of Missing Out, therefore they are so involved in so many activities, home care often suffers, leaving them feeling scattered and grumpy. It's best to either tap into that energetic, multitasking nature or use that innate talent for delegating. Like Tom Sawyer conning his friends into painting Aunt Polly's fence, a Gemini can rope anyone into doing anything.

Creating Inner Comfort: Those born under this sign love variety in their surroundings and regularly rearrange furnishings to stay stimulated. Yellow and pale green rooms also keep the Twins humming, especially if those rooms sport little sprigs of lily of the valley or big bunches of lavender—both Gemini-associated plants.

Life Outlook: What's next?

Kindred Spirits: Peter Pan, Sally Ride, Tim Allen, Marilyn Monroe, Isadora Duncan, Josephine Baker, Paul Gauguin, Che Guevara, Prince William, John F. Kennedy, Paul McCartney, Johnny Depp, Bob Dylan, Nicole Kidman, Liam Neeson, Cole Porter, Henri Rousseau, Frank Lloyd Wright, Donald Trump.

CANCER
June 22–July 22

Symbol: **THE CRAB**

In a Nutshell: Enigmatic. Emotional. Complex. That tough shell protects a soft and vulnerable heart.

Cleaning Style: Those born under Cancer are the caretakers of the zodiac, fussing over friends and family, though they tend to sidestep the care of floors and furnishings. Part of that avoidance is their known susceptibility to accidents; therefore, they must take particular care with ladders and machinery. Vacuum cleaners have been known to attack crabs.

Organizing Skills: Cancers have a true talent for organizing others but are slow to get their own acts together. Yet they need to, since they're such hoarders. A good closet system, adjustable shelves in every room and frequent evaluations of all that's stashed is a good start.

Creating Inner Comfort: The Crab may put on a tough act, growing back severed claws and all, but is so vulnerable and trusting, she needs a good security system, including an alert dog. Cancers prefer the old to the new—a battered farm table in the dining room and an old gate for a headboard—especially if surrounding walls are painted in watery hues of sea green and marine blue. The Crab's plants are water lily, sea grass and anything that grows in or near water.

Life Outlook: The straight road is direct, but the side street is more interesting.

Kindred Spirits: Alexander the Great, Frida Kahlo, the Dalai Lama, Julius Caesar, Princess Diana, Camilla Parker Bowles, Rembrandt, Ernest Hemingway, Meryl Streep, Nelson Mandela, Bill Cosby, Mark Chagall, Mary Baker Eddy, Tom Cruise, Phyllis Diller, Tom Hanks, Robin Williams.

LEO
July 22–August 23

Symbol: **THE LION**

In a Nutshell: Positive. Powerful. A true diva.

Organizing Skills: Leo is naturally organized but doesn't like dealing with the details of any job considered unworthy, including picking up the pieces of a project. That's what helpers are for, isn't it? Lions also form strong emotional attachments to things, so they must learn to keep only what supports and enhances their lives.

Cleaning Style: Since anything that smacks of the routine is beastly boring to the Lion, she needs to find creative ways to clean, preferably with someone she can talk, talk and talk some more to.

Better yet, get someone else to do the dirty work. If any sign is apt to hire professional cleaning help, this is it.

Creating Inner Comfort: Leos are people-loving people who like to indulge others in cushy comfort and dramatic trappings. Think thick Persian rugs, deep leather sofas and lots of ornately framed mirrors. Sunny colors of yellow, gold and topaz reflect Leo's upbeat nature, as do fields of sunflowers and scads of marigolds.

Life Outlook: My home is my castle, and I'm the reigning monarch.

Kindred Spirits: Martha Stewart, Whitney Houston, Napoleon, Arnold Schwarzenegger, Madonna, Sean Penn, Mata Hari, Bill Clinton, Jacqueline Kennedy Onassis, Antonio Banderas, Madame du Barry, Mick Jagger, Mae West, Benito Mussolini, Jennifer Lopez, Carl Jung, Cecil B. DeMille, Magic Johnson, Charlize Theron, Miss Piggy.

VIRGO
August 24–September 22

Symbol: **THE VIRGIN**

In a Nutshell: Modest. Directed. Fastidious.

Organizing Skills: With every shelf a still life and every drawer a military marvel, Virgos are so neat, they could create world order. But these totally tidy tendencies can be a bitch, even for them.

Cleaning Style: No one is cleaner than a Virgin. In fact, those born under this sign are so skilled at keeping their surroundings pure and pristine, they make the rest of us look like slackers. While all that spit and polish is admirable, sometimes it's good to lighten up and live a little. Even *Extra* Virgins need to have fun.

Creating Inner Comfort: A discriminating shopper with a dislike of all things ostentatious, a Virgo is the very soul of simplicity and is at her best when rooms are spare, orderly and accented in silver, indigo and purple. A few jelly jars sprouting sage or buttercups are Virginal mood lifters.

Life Outlook: If it's not on the list, it doesn't exist.

Kindred Spirits: Felix Unger, Betty Crocker, Mother Teresa, Maria Montessori, Miss Manners, Michael Jackson, Craig Claiborne, Queen Elizabeth I ("The Virgin Queen"), Grandma Moses, Goethe, Cameron Diaz, Salma Hayek, Keanu Reeves, Shania Twain, Tolstoy, Confucius, Richard Gere, Beyoncé.

LIBRA
September 22–October 22

Symbol: **THE SCALES**

In a Nutshell: Unflappable. Intelligent. Balanced.

Organizing Skills: Those born under the sign of the Scales are generally neat, but they can be indecisive when faced with choices, since they can see the arguments for both sides. "Should I keep this calculus book? It might come in handy someday." "What about this typewriter, in case the computer breaks down?" They also tend to procrastinate. "I'll worry about that tomorrow" is the Libra mantra.

Cleaning Style: Libras crave liberation from cleaning, especially heavy work and anything that might tip those golden scales they like to lug around. Luckily, they're charming delegators: "Come talk to me while I tidy up. Here, run this little rag around the room, will you?" Yet they'll not burden anyone with an unfair share of the load. Righteousness rules.

Creating Inner Comfort: Venus, goddess of all things elegant, influences Libra, so surroundings must be tasteful, almost to the point of obsession. Pale green, deep blue and shocking pink please a Libra, and hydrangeas and primroses soothe her sensitive soul. Light the candles and chill the Moët, Libra's in the limo, on her merry way.

Life Outlook: I'll worry about tomorrow, tomorrow.

Kindred Spirits: Scarlett O'Hara, Gwyneth Paltrow, Donna Karan, Ralph Lauren, John Lennon, Carrie Fisher, Paul Simon, Matt Damon, Oscar Wilde, Mohandas Gandhi, Sting, Luciano Pavarotti, Margaret Thatcher, Bruce Springsteen, Desmond Tutu, Stephen King, F. Scott Fitzgerald, Martina Navratilova, Catherine Zeta-Jones, Michael Douglas.

SCORPIO
October 23–November 21

Symbol: **THE SCORPION**

In a Nutshell: Intense. Determined. Passionate. Scorpios know what they want and use all their resources to get it.

Organizing Skills: Scorpios are compulsive organizers, tidying shelves and stacking stuff whether they're dressing for dinner or sinking into the tub. They have to. As collectors of everything from fine jewelry to chipped mugs, they must work harder than most at maintaining order.

Cleaning Style: Efficient and resourceful, a Scorpio can whip up a cheaper and better brew of floor polish or window cleaner than whatever you can find on the grocery store shelves. "You're using *what* to clean the drains? My dear, a little vinegar and baking soda will do the deed without the nasty fumes." This sign lives to clean.

Creating Inner Comforts: With those pinching claws and stinging tail, Scorpions come across as highly threatening, but plop them on a down sofa and wrap them in cashmere, and they'll put away their weapons. They might even turn into purring pussycats if they're surrounded by deep red walls and big bunches of white rhododendrons.

Life Outlook: Lord, please grant me patience. Now!

Kindred Spirits: Hillary Rodham Clinton, Marie Antoinette, Pablo Picasso, Whoopi Goldberg, Martin Luther, kd lang, Jodie Foster, Fran Lebowitz, Kevin Kline, Julia Roberts, Larry King, Albert Camus, Georgia O'Keeffe, Sylvia Plath, Christopher Columbus, Marie Curie, Dostoevsky, Bill Gates, Joaquin Phoenix, Kelly Osborne.

SAGITTARIUS
November 22–December 21

Symbol: **THE ARCHER**

In a Nutshell: Optimistic. Gregarious. Restless.

Organizing Skills: Time in the great outdoors is so important to those born under this sign, their homes must be kept as simple and pared as possible. This is fairly easy for Archers, since they have little attachment to worldly goods. They also have little patience for the mundane, like paying the mortgage and utility bills, which may send them out into the wild sooner than planned.

Cleaning Style: This whole-wheat wonder loves all things natural, but needs to be cautious about cleaning with organic homemade brews since they can breed sprouts in the shower and mushrooms in the doormat.

Creating Inner Comfort: The Archer is happiest in big, open, breeze-swept rooms and being surrounded by living things—pets, people and plants. She also also favors honest materials and unaffected style—woven grass rugs, denim upholstery and unadorned windows, especially if those windows overlook stands of birch or oak trees.

Life Outlook: Don't fence me in.

Kindred Spirits: Robin Hood, Lady Godiva, Tina Turner, Bruce Lee, Margaret Mead, Claude Levi-Strauss, Bette Midler, Louisa May Alcott, Charles Schulz, Mark Twain, Adam Clayton Powell, Jamie Lee Curtis, Steven Spielberg, Walt Disney, John Malkovich, Beethoven, Britney Spears.

CAPRICORN
December 22–January 20

Symbol: **THE GOAT**

In a Nutshell: Reserved. Goal oriented. Practical. Likes to chew on things before plodding onward and upward.

Organizing Skills: Capricorns hate conspicuous consumption, so you'll rarely find too many Jimmy Choos in the closet or too much caviar in the fridge. This sign is the most discriminating and disciplined of the zodiac, so whatever people or possessions are chosen to keep around, they're sure to be culled, sorted and labeled.

Cleaning Style: Ever-frugal Capricorns know that cleaning is the cheapest form of home improvement, so they dive into the Spic and Span with gusto and regularity. Not only that, they're fast, efficient and persistent—the superheroes of cleaning who are most likely to be inducted into the Housework Hall of Fame.

Creating Inner Comfort: As a dyed-in-the-wool (or angora) homebody, the Goat is happiest when surrounded by books, music and family. A few fine antiques define her traditionalist tendencies, provided they're inherited (read: free). Rich shades of chocolate, camel and coral ring the Goat's bell, and arrangements of pine, ivy and comfrey make her comfy.

Life Outlook: Steady progress leads to greener pastures.

Kindred Spirits: Joan of Arc, Mary Tyler Moore, Tiger Woods, Mao Tse-tung, Janis Joplin, J.R.R. Tolkien, Maggie Smith, Elizabeth Arden, Anthony Hopkins, Naomi Judd, Marlene Dietrich, Elvis

Presley, Rod Stewart, Tracey Ullman, Cokie Roberts, Ricky Martin, Geena Davis, Matt Lauer, Benjamin Franklin.

AQUARIUS
January 21–February 19

Symbol: **THE WATER BEARER**

In a Nutshell: Free-spirited. Imaginative. Unconventional. "Tell Aquarius he's crazy," advises Terry Marlowe in *Astrologically Incorrect*. "He gets off on it."

Organizing Skills: Excitement drives Aquarians, so unless they're stimulated by whatever they're arranging—jewels in the safe, designer duds in the closet or a tryst in the bedroom—they're bored stiff.

Cleaning Style: Remember Dave Delvechio's trick of cleaning his toilet with cola and a back brush? That's the Aquarian spirit of quirky innovation. Novelty is as necessary to this sign as air and water, since those born under it find the repetition of cleaning exceedingly tedious. Aquarians are known to motivate themselves with little rewards: a long soak in a scented tub, a white orchid on a newly cleared desk or a big mocha latte with double whipped cream savored while perusing the latest thriller.

Creating Inner Comfort: This air sign needs plenty of space, both literally and figuratively. She can find it by culling the possessions and people that no longer enhance her life. Aquarians also crave romance in their surroundings—a silk-draped canopy bed and soft tones of blue and rose.

Life Outlook: Imagination is intelligence at play.

Kindred spirits: Oprah Winfrey, Christie Brinkley, Placido Domingo, Alice Cooper, Lord Byron, Lewis Carroll, Mikhail Baryshnikov, Virginia Woolf, Justin Timberlake, Mozart, Robert Burns, Ayn Rand, Gertrude Stein, Charles Lindbergh, Charles Dickens, Galileo, Susan B. Anthony, Tom Brokaw, Chris Rock, Garth Brooks.

PISCES
February 20–March 20

Symbol: **THE FISH**

In a Nutshell: Highly evolved. Creative. Psychic.

Organizing Skills: Such sentimental souls, these fish. So hard for them to let go of the bait of possessions that keeps them out of the swim of things. That glut of goods can make surroundings as disorderly as a storm-tossed beach, but fish secretly crave the shipshape order of a schooner. Think built-in furnishings, adjustable shelves and transparent containers. Rethink the wisdom of saving broken fishing rods, rusty utensils and moldy anything.

Cleaning Style: Fish love clean water and have an understandable aversion to additives like detergent and toilet bowl cleaner. They're highly resourceful and imaginative, however, so whether they have the kids scoot around on towels polishing the floor, or have all their clothes laundered professionally, they'll find a way to get the job done.

Creating Inner Comforts: Pisces' sensual nature has her hooked on multijet showerheads, indoor *and* outdoor hot tubs, and fluffy Egyptian cotton towels. She also values peace and privacy and will go to great lengths to get it, building walls, adding screens and hiding under the covers. The splashing of a fountain or waterfall will keep the Fish serene as will liquid tones of aqua, violet and green.

Life Outlook: Catch me if you can.

Kindred Spirits: The Little Mermaid, Queen Latifah, Billy Crystal, Paris Hilton, Michelangelo, Elizabeth Taylor, Linus Pauling, Elizabeth Barrett Browning, Michael Jordan, Copernicus, Edna St. Vincent Millay, Glenn Close, Ansel Adams, Paula Zahn, Spike Lee, Michael Caine, Auguste Renoir.

- Medication consult:
    Lexapro
- Dr. Jacques
    2pm PhD. Psych.

x423   Tues. Jan 9 2pm
              Dr. Nancy Giles
              22 Mill St.
                 3rd floors. Ste308
           $1.50/hr. parking fee
    They'll call Pilgrim

CHAPTER SEVENTEEN

From Feng Shui to Fun's Way

*"Our homes are alive, pulsating with vibrations,
absorbing, storing and releasing energy."*

—Suzy Chiazzari,
The Healthy Home

*H*ee Chun's statesman husband left her for a mistress shortly
after she gave birth to their daughter, despite the fact that she was
young, beautiful and highborn. Even with a dutiful daughter and a
healthy inheritance, illness and misfortune followed my husband's
maternal grandmother all her life. Why? Some would speculate that
her surroundings lacked good chi—the energy that purportedly
promotes good fortune.

Far-fetched? Maybe. But a good portion of the world believes in
the cultivation of good chi, arranging surroundings in such a way to
capture chi and encourage its beneficial flow. Flowing chi is happy
chi, and happy chi makes happy campers.

Feng shui (pronounced *fung shway*), a mystical mix of design and
placement, is the traditional way of cultivating good chi. However,
with its inscrutable formulas and cosmic calculations, it has become

way too complicated. Yet at one time, it was all so simple.

> "A feeling of spaciousness is determined more by energy flow than it is by square feet."
>
> —Billy Baldwin, interior designer

Thousands of years ago in Asia, where it all began, people observed that the flow of wind (feng) and water (shui) could produce an extraordinary form of energy. They discovered when they tweaked their surroundings a certain way, they could capture this vibe and, in turn, increase their luck, or more accurately, their successes and well-being. Positioning a home on the slope of a hill, for example, encouraged good chi, since it provided a breeze and protection from gales. If the slope was sunny, the home was cheerful. If the home faced water, crops could be irrigated and animals grazed. If the home had a view, danger could be spotted. If it was easy to keep clean, there were fewer germs, and, in turn, fewer illnesses. Thus, its inhabitants not only survived, they thrived.

Much of this positioning is instinctive today. When we choose a seat in a restaurant, we gravitate to one with its back to the protective wall. We're drawn to greenery because it offers protection in the wild. We love a crackling fire in the hearth for much the same reason. We respond to the warmth of the sun as well as to the sound and sight of flowing water, since they're the source of all life.

These instincts are the core of feng shui. But over the centuries, the discipline has taken on so many rules and taboos, you need a shaman to interpret them. But Fun's Way—feng shui's newest, simplest and most playful offshoot—gets back to the heart of the matter with its simple, natural and fun approach to good living.

The Fun Way

Practicing Fun's Way is like placing stones in a stream. The stones not only change the look and sound of the stream, they also force it to splash up around the rocks, creating bubbles, mists and rainbows. The stones may also divert the water to a whole new course or cause the stream to pool. Too many stones in the stream, and it stagnates. Too few and it may flood. In all cases, the stones change the life around them.

Our possessions are the stones in the stream. They affect the order, light, air, sound and very soul of our surroundings. Once we learn to arrange, balance and sometimes toss these stones, we can enjoy all the benefits we can handle.

Cultivate Good Chi

We don't need to build a house on a hill or graze goats on the lawn to increase our health, happiness and good hair days. Fun's Way offers easier ways to attract good chi and keep it flowing.

- **Welcome chi inside with an inviting entry.** When Sam Garcia and Bernie Freeborn bought a neglected bungalow in the Hillcrest neighborhood of San Diego, the first thing they did was paint the front door French blue and install pewter hardware. They then planted morning glories to frame the tiny front porch. "I'm not sure if it's Fun's Way or even feng shui," said Bernie. "But I do know the new entry hugs me every time I walk up the front steps."

- **Create a break.** Bernie and Sam opened the door to good chi by dividing the living room from the front door with a waist-high wall that provides a place of transition between outside and inside without blocking natural light. The new foyer also encourages chi to slow down and ramble through rooms rather than whip in one door and out the other.

> "You want chi to meander around a room like a refreshing breeze, rather than blowing straight through like a strong wind."
>
> —Terah Kathryn Collins,
> *The Western Guide to Feng Shui*

Let It Flow

✂ Like towns and cities, chi functions best with free traffic flow. Make sure the major arteries that run from room to room are clear of clutter, furnishings and other bottlenecks. I found that just removing the end chair from our dining table cleared the heavily used path through the room to the kitchen.

✂ All doors should swing freely. Clear any clogs, making sure swing space is at least the width of the door. Sam and Bernie found space so tight in their circa 1928 home, they replaced a couple of interior doors with less-intrusive drapery panels. "It's great to close the draperies when the kitchen's a mess," said Sam. "And they give the room a soft, cozy feeling."

✂ Since eating and sleeping are basic to our well-being, make it a point to keep the space on and around the bed, the kitchen counter and the family dining table debris free.

Funswaytional Furnishing

❀ People are most comfortable when they're at slight angles to each other rather than in full frontal mode, so create loose circles of seating in well-defined areas, such as in front of a fireplace and around the coffee table. Tighten the circle enough so that traffic passes around, not through it, but keep it open enough for graceful access and exits.

❀ Fun's Way likes a variety of seating options so various physical and psychological needs are met. An ottoman or a bench is conducive to perching and circulating, an easy chair is good for settling in and a rocker lulls one into a state of serenity.

❀ Ensure that each person has a decent view of the surroundings when dining. Seeing the toilet, litter box or a sink full of greasy pans makes chi queasy.

Create Romance

⌂ Like many of us, chi is forgetful and sometimes needs to be reminded of its purpose in the bedroom—rest and romance. Give it a boost by dressing the bed in an orgy of comfort: crisp cotton sheets in the summer, fuzzy flannel ones in the winter, a fat comforter, a soft throw and the best pillows a budget can buy. Make sure to pull it together every morning. An unmade bed depresses chi.

> "The bedroom contains unfathomable mysteries and power."
>
> —Anthony Lawlor,
> *A Home for the Soul*

⚖ If you're pretty in pink or glow in gold, liberally decorate with that color. Lin Yu, a dazzling courtesan of the Ming dynasty, had her private rooms lined with coral and ivory silk to reflect her peaches-and-cream complexion. She also had bronze screens studded with topaz and amber stones to compliment her gold-flecked eyes.

⚖ An Oriental rug adds a rich splash of color and warmth to a bedroom, but avoid one with a hunting design. The Persians have long held that while a hunting scene rug adds energy to almost any room in the house, it brings conflict to a bedroom.

⚖ Seeking a new relationship? Remove all things associated with an old one. Reminders of the past keep us from moving ahead. When we make room for growth, love blossoms.

⚖ Display pictures of loving couples to either cement a relationship or find a new one. I know a woman who made a "wish collage" of couples walking on the beach, playing tennis and cooking together. On it she superimposed a list of all the qualities she was looking for in a guy, then hung the  whole thing across from her bed. She met the man of her dreams in less than a month and married him a year later. She credits the collage. "On a practical level, words and pictures help you zero in on what you're looking for, so you're more apt to recognize it," she said. "But I believe there's more to it than that. When you put thought and love into something like this, you send a message to the universe. And the universe always responds."

Sweet Dreams

❀ Move workout and office equipment out of the bedroom. Complete rest is nearly impossible when unpaid bills and the stationary bike beckon. One Fun's Way follower moved her rower and her desk to a corner of her living room. When company comes, she simply hides the equipment with a portable screen. "My living room sat empty most of the time anyway," she said. "Now that I've put it to work, my bedroom is my sanctuary."

❀ Clear the bedroom of chi-clogging clutter by shelving books and magazines and corralling the music system, TV and DVDs in a sleek cabinet. Clear space is a tranquil place.

❀ Decorate with soft colors. Soothing shades of lilac, green and blue are restful in a bedroom, while the vibrations of bright primary colors keep us tossing and turning, even in the dark. My husband and I once checked into a Las Vegas hotel room that was such a riot of color, it was obviously designed to get its occupants into the casino. It worked. We were so wired, we hardly slept.

❀ Create the darkness your body craves with window coverings that completely block out light. Bernie and Sam hung lined shades in their bedroom so they extend above and beyond the window frame. "We're across the street from a brightly lit club," said Sam. "So blackout fabric is critical."

❀ Before drifting off for the night, reflect on the day. Instead of brooding over today's problems or tomorrow's projects, recall the three best things that happened. I find that blessings are always there if I look for them, and gratitude improves my attitude.

A Beneficial Bathroom

↤ To maintain harmony with your beloved, maintain separate bathrooms if possible. Standards of cleanliness and modesty are rarely equal, and chi hates squabbling.

↤ Fun's Way followers find that lighting a scented candle helps sweeten chi's cosmic breath, which can get a little ripe in the morning. Striking a match is effective too.

> "Bathrooms are often a big source of trouble. It may not look like it, but the loo is the place where you can easily lose your man down the pan if you're not careful."
>
> —Sarah Bartlett,
> Feng Shui for Lovers

↤ Increase good hair days by always storing your hairdryer, styling brush and products together so they develop a harmonious relationship. Toss those ratty scrunchies, broken combs and dated hairpieces while you're at it.

↤ Always lower the toilet lid after each use and train others to do the same. Keeping the lid closed has three benefits: (1) It protects chi from being sucked away; (2) it prevents airborne bacteria from spewing through the room while flushing; and (3) it protects female users from dead-of-night dousings.

HISTORICAL DIRT

The Legend of Wind and Water

According to traditional feng shui teachings, chi is in constant danger of getting sucked down the toilet, taking our loot and luck with it.

"Never have a toilet at the end of the hallway," warns the feng shui master, and "For heaven's sake, keep the door shut and the lid down!" (Feng shui masters often sound like moms.)

How did this vixen and victim relationship come about? Fun's Way has a theory that I now reveal for the first time:

Once upon a time, Wind was a gentle breeze and Water was as smooth as a bolt of blue silk. But Wind got bored with this placid life and decided to test his yang. So he puffed his cheeks and blew across Water. Water didn't mind at first, since she was very yin and frankly was a little tired of being so flat. In fact, she rather liked the cool tickle of ripples across her usually calm surface.

"This is fun," thought Wind as he huffed harder, tossing Water first into gray waves then into towering white caps.

"That's enough, Wind," said Water nervously.

But Wind was feeling very powerful, so he puffed and roared and then howled across the seven seas. Hurricanes raged, tsunamis spouted and typhoons churned Water until she scraped her sandy bottom and threw up all her fish. But she could not get Wind to stop.

"This must cease," gasped Water. "I must find a way to harness my own power." So she focused very hard until she sucked Wind from the heavens. Down spun Wind into the roiling whirlpool until he scoured the deepest caverns of the ocean.

"Stop!" cried Wind. "I'm drowning!"

"I'll let you go," said Water, "if you promise to control yourself and not be so damned yang."

"I promise," promised Wind.

So Water released Wind, and they became friends once
more. But Water never quite forgave nor trusted Wind again.
Which is why she likes to teach him a lesson every so often by
luring him into the bathroom and sucking him into her domestic
vortex—the toilet.

All Through the House

❁ Blessed with an ample, well-rounded body? Hang art that
celebrates your voluptuousness. Nudes by Botero, Rubens and
Gauguin glorify the full form.

❁ Whether buying a piece of furniture
or laying out a flowerbed, choose
curves over straight lines. An
oval desk inspires creativity, a
winding path invites explo-
ration and a round table promotes good conversation. And
unlike a rectangular table, you
can always squeeze another diner
around a round one.

"Leave an open window
when you go on vacation,
and when you return, you
will find that the problems of
a cluttered living space will
have resolved themselves."

—Rohan Candappa, *Wrong Shui*

❁ Grow the right greenery. Chi favors houseplants with gentle,
rounded shapes like African violets and kalanchoe, but hates
plants with swordlike shapes that poke it as it swirls about.
Injured chi is angry chi, and angry chi can turn on you.

✿ Hang uplifting art. Sunlit landscapes, botanical prints and smiling portraits are cheerful, while pictures of battles, bleak cityscapes and sad-looking people charge a space with negative energy.

✿ Cover hard edges with soft fabric. Nightstands, tables, windows, headboards and even walls can create a cocoon of coziness when they're draped in fabric. Fabric also muffles noise like a blanket of snow.

✿ Fire sparks energy in a room, drawing in good chi. If you have a fireplace, use it often. If not, light candles. I keep a little brass candle-lamp on the desk near my kitchen table. I move it to the table and light it any time the weather is dark or gloomy. It's amazing how much cheer it brings to the room, especially on a cold rainy night.

✿ Children stimulate chi, so always have a few around, preferably someone else's so you can send them home when the chi gets hyperactive.

✿ Avoid keeping a caged bird, since it symbolizes an inability to fly and reach one's ambitions. Besides, a caged bird makes an inauspicious mess.

"Never position a rock near a hard place."
—Rohan Candappa

✿ Keep cleaning equipment hidden. It's considered by some to be unlucky. On second thought, hire a cleaning service that brings its own equipment.

CLEANING WITH FENG SHUI

As an avid gardener, Ann Marie Holmes was drawn to Findhorn, an ecovillage on the coast of northern Scotland, known for its spiritual approach to gardening.

"As I was meditating there one day, I got a sense that there was a life force in buildings as well as in plants," said Holmes. "So I ran to personnel and told them that as an interior designer, I had to explore this."

"Personnel said, 'That's 'Cleaning.'"

"No, no, that's too mundane," countered Holmes. But she ended up as cleaning manager.

What Holmes discovered as chief cleaner was that true intention and a positive attitude can produce extraordinary results in a space.

"It wasn't so much *what* we did, it was *how* we did it," explained Holmes. "We taught people to let go of the old concepts of cleaning and explained that as cleaners, we're agents of change. There is a reason witches ride brooms, as far as I'm concerned. They're magical. Brooms transform places."

The cleaning department, said Holmes, went from a place that others would avoid at all costs to one that attracted a waiting list of volunteers. When visitors wanted to get a sense of Findhorn, they were sent to Cleaning.

Take the New Zealand businessman. He had only three days to get the essence of the place, so he was sent to Cleaning.

"He arrived in a three-piece suit, and we sent him to the men's loo, suggesting he talk to the toilets as he scrubbed them," she said. "He came back elated, saying how he approached each toilet as something valuable. He believed he found the meaning of life in a piece of dust."

The whole experience led Holmes to study feng shui and become a practitioner once she arrived back in the states.

> "There was more going on than I could explain," she said. "There's something about dusting, rearranging things and moving energy that settles your life. Feng shui puts words to that.
>
> "I believe when we set out to bring order and balance to the environment, it brings order and balance into our own lives."

Psychic Health

Fun's Way can enhance our inner as well as our outer comfort.

⚳ Headache prone? Try a worry stone. Find a smooth, flat, oval-shaped stone by a body of water. Gently stroke it three times in a circular motion, and then hold it to your forehead for thirty seconds, mentally depositing troubled thoughts into the stone. Release it, and slowly drink an eight-ounce glass of room-temperature water, then hold the stone to your forehead another thirty seconds. Rinse and dry the stone, place it in your medicine cabinet and enjoy the rest of the day.

⚳ After a major clutter clearing, clean the stagnant energy it may have left behind by burning a "smudge stick," a tied clump of dried sage or lavender (found in many natural food stores). Light it at one end to burn off negative energy and impart a pleasant scent. Smolder it in a fireplace, a large

"An interior is the natural projection of the soul."
—Coco Chanel

seashell or metal tray and stay with it to the end to make the process both mindful and safe.

🪝 Shampoo regret, resentment and other counterproductive emotions from your psyche right along with old hairspray and mousse. As you lather up, consider any negativity you may be harboring in your head. When it's time to rinse, release it down the drain with the suds. Massage in a bit of conditioner for healing. When the water runs clear, your spirit can too.

🪝 Gather friends for a "wish stick" ritual. On New Year's Eve, a group of our friends gathers to discard what we don't want in our lives and encourage what we do. After dinner, we each select two wooden chopsticks from the center of the table, where slips of paper, pens, tape, ribbon, feathers and other bits of fluff are also placed. We write whatever it is we want to get rid of—tangible or abstract—during the coming year on a slip of paper and roll and tape it around one "wish stick." We then write whatever good we want to foster and wrap it around the other. We decorate them both, then ceremoniously walk to the fireplace as a group, silently saying a prayer or affirmation, and toss the negative stick into the fire and watch it burn. We take the other stick home and plant it in the soil of the yard or a houseplant "to grow."

> "May the force be with you."
>
> —Obi-Wan Kenobi

LIFE MATTERS:

Sharing Abundance

Abundance is a beautiful thing, especially when it encompasses friends, family, flowers, fresh air and generosity in one's heart.

One of the easiest ways to create a sense of abundance is by piling a bowl with fresh, seasonal fruit and placing it somewhere prominent. But don't just admire it. Share it.

Sounds simple, no? Not when display is the end-all.

When my parents were going through hard times with a fifth child on the way, they asked a rich but rather anal relative to babysit the four oldest kids when my mother went into labor. When my father picked up the boys that night, my aunt was livid that they were so badly behaved they actually *ate* all of the fruit she had so artistically arranged in a silver bowl on the table.

When show takes precedence over generosity, chi flees.

DESIGN FOR LIVING

The Yin and the Yang of Color

Always add a little yang (active-masculine) color to a yin (passive-feminine) room. A soft blue den, for instance, benefits from a shot of red or bright yellow in the form of pillows, flowering plants, lampshades or other accessories. A sage green office is soothing, but a little peach will warm it and keep the working chi active and flowing.

CHAPTER EIGHTEEN

Subliminal Mood Lifters

*"Enjoy the little things; for one day
you may look back and realize
they were the big things."*

—Robert Brault, writer

The old place was a musty, dusty, barely habitable hut when the family creaked open its weathered door in early June. But by Independence Day, pitchers of wildflowers decorated tables, pastel flannel sheets covered the dark and worn upholstery, pink paper lanterns hid the ugly ceiling fixtures and window boxes cascaded roses that would perfume the air throughout the summer.

"Our Cape Cod cottage wasn't nearly as nice as our year-round home, but it always made me feel good," said Beth Sullivan. "It wasn't just a vacation thing or that my sister and I could sweep the sand through the floor boards. It was the way my mom could quickly transform an almost spooky place into something so warm and pretty that we were all buoyed by it. It was a Cinderella process that seemed magical to me."

The power of environmental mood lifting had such a powerful influence on Beth, she made a career of it, but not in the traditional fabric and floor plan sense. Instead, Beth stages homes for sellers with scent, sound and other subliminal elements to pull both heart and purse strings.

> "Take whatever steps are necessary to make the places you spend time in as inspiring, beautiful and liberating for your spirit as possible."
> —Elaine Saint James,
> *Inner Simplicity*

Like Beth, I've long been affected by my environment, but as a conventionally trained interior designer, I believed that mood-boosting surroundings needed a good dose of effort, time and cash. A weekend environmental design seminar changed all that.

The first night, our group of twelve from various walks of life met in a cavernous room lit by overhead fluorescent lights and furnished with metal folding tables, their matching chairs and a battered sofa. A couple of floor lamps stood in one corner of the room, an empty fireplace in the other and a few badly hung pictures adorned the stark white walls. It was a bleak backdrop to what I hoped would be a promising seminar.

We settled in for a slide show. Instead, we got some action. Architect and *Healing Environments* author Carol Venolia gave us an assignment: Transform the dreary space into a cozy, welcoming one. It was surprising to see how instinctive it was for all of us. Two of us dragged the sofa over to the fireplace, flanked it with the floor lamps and formed a semicircle with the other chairs. Others gathered fallen leaves and branches from the yard for the fireplace. One of the larger pictures was removed from its too-high hook and propped on the mantel. We lit the fire, turned off the overheads and turned on the reading lamps. Someone threw her cashmere shawl over the sofa, and abracadabra—we had created a warm, welcoming, uplifting space out of a cheerless one. Time: 16 minutes. Cost: zero. Mood-boosting factor: mammoth.

I'm now a believer. The following inexpensive, simple techniques for warming a home and lifting the spirit may make you a believer too.

"Comfort is perhaps the ultimate luxury."
—Billy Baldwin

Integrate Nature

From Moses to Muhammad, when ancient prophets needed solace and encouragement, they sought it in the wilderness. But few of us have the time or the resources to sit in the backyard, let alone on a mountain. We spend most of our time indoors at work, in the car and at home, cut off from the great outdoors. Yet there are easy ways to bring nature's mood-boosting powers inside.

✿ Open the house to the outdoors whenever possible. "We may not be able to do that all year," said Carol Venolia. "But there are days when we can keep the windows open and let the breeze blow through. It's important to reconnect with the cycles of nature, to feel the wind and the temperature changes, and to notice the daily and seasonal patterns of the sun. Connecting with nature from even indoors reminds us that we belong to the larger scheme of things."

"Our homes have to be havens of light, joy and air."
—Alexandra Stoddard

✿ Be in the light. Science is rediscovering light's healing powers and is using it as a tool in treating conditions like PMS, sleep disorders and depression. Studies at the University of British Columbia indicate that exposure to outdoor early morning light can lessen the effects of PMS by 60 percent. At the

University of California, San Diego, light-therapy researcher Dr. Daniel Kripke treats depression and sleep disorders by dosing patients with both natural and artificial light. "As a general rule," explained Kripke, "the more light these patients receive, the more likely they are to feel better."

❀ Get to know your feathered friends by attaching a bird feeder to a window. "Even if you're a number of stories up in an apartment building, it's a fun way to interact with nature," said Carol Venolia. Keeping a field guide of local birds by the window will help you identify them.

NATURE AND STRESS

According to a Cornell University study of 337 children in grades three to five, those in homes with natural elements inside (including plants, flowers and pets) appeared to be less affected by stress in their lives.

Practice Plant Therapy

Houseplants are like perfect babies: They're pretty, they respond to care and other than leaking every so often, they're mostly well behaved.

🌱 Add color, moisture and oxygen to rooms with a few flowering, easy growers like kalanchoe, a succulent that blooms for months and comes in a rainbow of hues. Bromeliads, amaryllis and peace lily are also robust room brighteners.

⅃ Brown thumb? Interior redesigner Marie
Kinnaman advises her clients to buy their
houseplants at Home Depot, where the
store replaces dead and dying plants up
to a full year from the purchase date. "Just
keep the receipt in a resealable sandwich
bag under the pot, so you won't lose it,"
advises Kinnaman. "Plants add so much life to a room, yet so
many homes lack them."

> "Flowers
> are nature's
> courtesans."
> —Ilse Crawford,
> *The Sensual Home*

⅃ Place a few water-filled jars of favorite herbs on the kitchen
counter to snip into salads, soups and sauces. Herbs not only
add a fresh and homey look, they're conveniently
close on a counter.

Flower Power

> "Find paradise
> where you are."
> —Carol Venolia

Behavioral studies at Rutgers University found
that the presence of flowers triggers happy emotions, boosts feelings of satisfaction and stimulates
social interaction. But most of us don't need a scientific study to
know that flowers just feel good. A few easy ways to always have
them around:

❀ Grow or buy varieties with staying power. According to the
American Society of Florists, anthurium, carnation, alstroe-
meria, delphinium and most lilies can last up to two
weeks if treated with tender loving care. TLC includes
removing leaves below the water line, changing the water
every other day, using floral preservative and keeping
flowers away from heating vents and direct sunlight.

- We don't need armfuls of blossoms to boost our mood. One perfect posy or fern sprig in a pretty bud vase by the kitchen sink will brighten the dishwashing routine. Or place it on a desk to lighten paperwork.

"If only the sun would come out, I would have this score finished in no time."
—Richard Wagner, composer

- Launch three perfect flower heads in a wide and shallow glass bowl. Flat blooms, like gerbera daisies, mums and gardenias, are better floaters than bell-shaped blossoms, like tulips and lilies. Add a couple of floating candles for a nighttime glow.

- Celebrate the seasons on the kitchen table. I often center a dish of seashells in the summer, a bowl of apples in the fall, a basket of pinecones in the winter and a pitcher of tulips in the spring to connect me with nature's time line.

Scent Your Sanctuary

- Know what scents make you happiest. "Often the fragrances that smell best to us evoke pleasant memories of childhood," explains Marie Kinnaman. The interior redesigner carries scented linen spray and laundry detergent aptly named Pure Grass, Beach House and Paris Rain in her At Home on Main Street shop in Fallbrook, California. "A fresh and clean-smelling home is always better than a perfumey one," maintains Kinnaman.

- Sleep with the fresh scent of sunlight by drying or airing sheets, blankets and pillows in the sun. Clotheslines are banned in many neighborhoods, but Beth Sullivan gets around the rule by laying her damp-from-the-dryer sheets over a wide patch of rosemary and sage in her Tucson backyard. "I've always loved the smell of sun-dried sheets, but the herbs add something extra special," she said. "I just have to anchor their corners with stones so they don't blow away; though I finally met my neighbor when I asked to retrieve a sheet from her yard."

> "The quickest way to change someone's mood is to change the smell of their surroundings."
>
> —Alan Hirsch, M.D.,
> Smell and Taste Treatment
> and Research Foundation

⚓ Fill the house with the aroma of baking even if you're just opening a can of soup. Drizzle a head of garlic with olive oil and bake it at 350 degrees for about a half hour. Squeeze each clove directly on bread for a buttery, flavorful spread. Or bake frozen dough for the aroma of homemade heaven.

⚓ Keep fresh air circulating through the car by keeping the windows cracked when parked in the garage. Tuck a fabric softener sheet in the back pouch of a car seat as well for a fresh scent.

⚓ Tie a fistful of eucalyptus branches with ribbon or raffia and hang them from a hook near the shower or tub. The hot steam will release the tree's woodsy, head-clearing fragrance.

⚓ Place a bouquet of lavender on your nightstand or wedge a sachet of it between the headboard and wall. The springtime scent has long been believed to induce sleep and inspire sweet dreams.

⚘ Plant a bedroom window box or nearby patio pot with something aromatic, like nicotiana or gardenia, so the scent drifts inside through the night. We planted night-blooming jasmine outside our guest room window that has lulled many a sleeper into a fragrant dreamland.

Boost Comfort

Though we're not always conscious of it, comfort, or lack of it, affects our mood. As Goldilocks discovered, a good, supportive chair cradles and buoys, while an uncomfortable one can be a literal pain in the butt. Even the look of comfort affects how we feel.

❀ A room looks warmer, feels cushier and is quieter when there's more fabric and padding than there is wood, glass, stone and metal. Skirt a table, frame window blinds with drapery panels and top bare benches and chairs with plump seat cushions.

❀ Consider the physical needs of the household before investing in furniture. Your tall spouse may be most comfortable in a chair with an extra deep seat cushion. Granny may need sturdy arms on a dining room chair to rise from it easily. Your preschooler may feel more secure with a footstool under the kitchen table.

> "Comfort, physical comfort, is wall-to-wall carpeting, lots of sofas and chairs and everything very clean."
>
> —Fran Lebowitz, writer

❀ Regard the comforting potential of a rocker. When the Charlotte/Douglas International Airport in Charlotte, North

Carolina, moved twenty rocking chairs into their passenger lounges for a 1997 art exhibit, frazzled travelers flocked to them. The rocker fleet has doubled since, with plans for more. "The rocker gives a great sense of place since it's long been associated with the Southern comfort of the front porch," said public affairs assistant Jennifer Shouse. "From all the positive feedback we're getting, we know passengers love them."

❀ If there's space, move an upholstered chair into a home office, master bedroom, kitchen or child's room. Place it near the window for quality reading and comfy daydreaming.

❀ Keep an ottoman paired to a chair. "I see so many people separate the two, putting the ottoman on the other side of the coffee table, so they can't really use it as a footstool," said Marie Kinnaman. "But an ottoman adds so much comfort to a chair when we need to put our feet up at the end of the day."

> "The furniture looks so classic, but it's overstuffed, oversized and soft, so you just slouch into everything. That kind of ease, to me, is sexy."
> —Vera Wang, fashion designer, describing her own home

❀ Boost sofa comfort with a couple of big bolster pillows. These fat sausages can function as neck or foot support for a couch potato, spine support for a sloucher or portable armrests for someone stuck in the middle seat. A bolster or two on the bed is also good for reading or watching TV.

❀ Remember that the primary purpose of a sofa is for sitting and stretching out, not to showcase decorative pillows. When the sofa is decked out with dozens of little pillows, it's a challenge to settle in, especially when those pillows are studded with trendy buttons, beads and other anatomy pokers.

✿ Adopt a "blankie." A small, soft throw is perfect for curling up with a book or someone you love, including yourself.

> "This chair is like a woman: big hips, short legs. It says 'Come sit on my lap.'"
> —Barbara Barry, furniture designer

Tame Technology

> "Declare a happiness day. Do whatever makes you feel good, useful and fulfilled. Save unpleasant tasks, difficult people and negative thoughts for tomorrow."
> —March calendar, *Oprah* magazine

San Diego Union-Tribune writer Richard Louv tells the tale of a physician/environmentalist whose wife asked him if he thought it was about to rain. "Let me check," said the doctor, as he rose from his chair, turned on the computer and opened the local weather site. As he tapped away on the keyboard, his wife opened the door, stuck out her hand and announced, "It's raining."

Technology is distancing us so far from opening the door to life, we've almost forgotten how to do it. In the process, we're losing touch with nature, as well as the ability to relate to others, unless of course, it's online.

The technogenie has grown too big to stuff back into his bottle, but there are ways to keep him from completely dominating our lives.

 Substitute a chunk of TV and online time with a project you've always wanted to try, like painting, furniture refinishing or learning how to bake bread. Creativity is always more satisfying than passivity.

Replace a night of crime shows, news broadcasts and dysfunctional family sitcoms with upbeat comedy, movie classics and home-improvement shows. Negativity, even if it's only dramatized, is dispiriting.

Consider reading the news rather than watching it. Disturbing news is more so when it's accompanied by in-your-face images and all-too-real noise. A newspaper or newsmagazine, on the other hand, can be scanned in about the same time it takes to watch a half hour of commercial-filled TV news. Plus we can decide what *we* deem newsworthy.

Take a total newsbreak for a day or more; then ask yourself if it's more important to be informed or relaxed. There's not a lot we can do about murder and mayhem, but we can make our inner world a calmer place by tuning out negativity. No news is often good news.

Have a family "blackout night." Can the computer, the TV and other technological intrusions, and dine only by candle and firelight. Tell ghost stories, or if that's too scary, swap tales about how people might have played, eaten and got along before electricity.

"The final test of any room is when you can curl up and read a book in it."
—Charlotte Moss, New York interior designer

⚲ Turn off the cell phone, beeper and fax every so often. Turn down the answering machine as well, so it silently screens messages. No one has to be available 24/7, yet it's a habit we've all fallen into.

"Focus on what you are grateful for and the gods will heap more goodies upon you."
—Karen Kingston, *Clear Your Clutter with Feng Shui*

LIFE MATTERS:

Know What You Love

What lifts your mood is likely different from what lifts the mood of someone else. "There are some universals," explains Carol Venolia, "but what's really magical is when someone has done a little self-analysis and says something like: 'It's yellow daffodils! That's what does it for me!'

"It may not be 'yellow daffodils' for everybody, but it'll be that one thing that makes us go 'ahhh' because it reminds us of childhood or some other happy time.

"The one thing to remember," stresses Venolia, "is that any time you carry out an environmental improvement—no matter how small—you achieve not only a physical result but also enduring evidence of your ability to change the world for the better."

CHAPTER NINETEEN

Giving Your Home Heart and Soul

"A house itself isn't important,
it's what you do in it, how you give it life."

—Donatella Versace, fashion designer

The qualities we want in a partner—good looks, charm and low maintenance—are the same qualities we want in a home. The big advantage of a home, however, is that we can mold it into exactly what we want and make it reflect the best of who we are. Tricky business with a partner, but definitely doable with a home.

Please Yourself

Decorating to impress others is a waste of time, maintains architect Christopher Alexander. The architect and coauthor of the classic *A Pattern Language* believes that we should surround ourselves with things that warm the heart and validate our values. But most of us, he says, decorate

"To thine own self be true."

—William Shakespeare

with the fashionable things we think will please others. "The irony is," he wrote, "the visitors who come into a room don't want this nonsense any more than the people who live there. It is far more fascinating to come into a room which is the living expression of a person, or a group of people, so that you can see their lives, their histories, their inclinations."

Show Your Passion

"If you really love those dishtowels you found at Williams-Sonoma, buy a whole box of them and make little tab curtains for your kitchen," offers interior designer and author Alexandra Stoddard. "If they make you happy doing the dishes, they'll make you happier hanging at your window."

Stoddard finds that many of us stash away the very things that say the most about us. One of her clients had hidden away dozens of needlework pillows that she had made over the years. "She didn't think they were worthy," said Stoddard. "But they were beautiful."

> "It is the sweet, simple things of life which are the real ones after all."
> —Laura Ingalls Wilder, writer

Since the client loved gardening and had worked most of the pillows in flower motifs, the designer painted her client's walls soft green, her ceiling sky blue and the woodwork glossy white. She then filled the walls with framed botanical prints and scattered the once-closeted pillows on sofas and chairs. The former living room is now the new "garden room."

Another client of Stoddard's had no art at all. What she did have were scads of Emilio Pucci silk scarves. "She loved them, but they were so expensive, she thought they were too good to wear, so they sat folded in a dark closet," said Stoddard. "I said 'Let there be light' and had them all framed."

Stoddard believes that even tra-ditional art can be displayed with imagination and verve if it's truly loved. She and her husband, Peter, have a number of watercolors and oils by French artist Roger Muhl dis-played throughout their Connecticut home. They've also clipped images from the artist's catalog, encased them in stock frames and hung them under their free-standing bathroom sink so they can enjoy them from the tub as they bathe. Says Stoddard, "To be in a house that is filled with who we are and what we love is such a blessing."

> "I always pick blue gingham if available. Blue gingham constellates a galaxy of memories (beach, ocean, the first place-mats in my first house) that confirm me."
>
> —Phyllis Theroux, writer

COLLECTIONS AND GENDER

Social scientists have long believed that personal collections, the things we choose to keep around and display to others, define who we are and what we value.

What may be surprising, however, is what we choose to collect is often determined by our gender.

According to a joint study at the Universities of Utah and Arizona, men tend to collect images of power—cars, weapons and sports items. Women, however, are drawn to the diminutive and the domestic—animal replicas, dolls and china.

Have the Courage of Your Convictions

Not long ago, I helped my daughter Kelley decorate her new apartment by coordinating a hand-me-down rust sofa with an old Persian rug, a camel-colored chair, some kilim pillows and a Chagall print. We were both happy with the results, but she wanted to find something "big and beautiful" for a prominent wall that faced the entry and the living room. "Whatever rings your bell," I said, assuming we shared the same bell. A few weeks later, when I dropped by, I was nearly knocked flat by a huge neon pink and chrome yellow *Endless Summer* movie poster. I wanted to yell, "You could at least move it to the privacy of your bedroom!" but held my tongue.

> "Your home is the most revealing aspect of your inner growth and your ability to see beauty."
> —Alexandra Stoddard

But you know what? Since it reflects her surf-goddess lifestyle better than some terribly tasteful museum poster that I had in mind, it not only works, it's truly her.

Forget Fads

> "There is no right or wrong when it comes to arranging your own home, but you will be happier if you make decisions that come from your own heart."
> —Gary Thorpe, *Sweeping Changes*

Fads are fun, but they're signs of the times that hold no deeper meaning than a desire to be hip. What's wrong with hip? Not a thing when we're talking skirt length or pant flare, but following furnishing fads too closely not only dates a place, it makes it less "us" and more "them."

Even the trendsetters avoid being too hip at home. When everyone else went spare and sleek in the 1930s, Coco Chanel filled her Paris apartment with exotic and unlikely objects from her world travels.

Vogue editor Diana Vreeland surrounded herself with scarlet walls and furnishings when the rest of the world was deep into earth tones.

> "Fashion changes— style remains."
> —Coco Chanel

Psychoanalyst Carl Jung covered the stone walls of his study with sketches of dream images, thoughts and mandalas, because they were far more fascinating to him than anything he could buy.

Robert Redford chose Native American art and rustic furnishings long before they were fashionable and continues to do so because of his strong affinity for Western American culture.

Give It Your Best Shot

My childhood friend Lynne Moretti has one of the most personal guest rooms I've ever had the pleasure of staying in. She's framed a few generations of family snapshots, all taken in the old town of Weymouth, Massachusetts, and hung them on all four walls. I've found it fascinating to peruse the collection before turning in; just think of how fun it must be for a visiting relative.

Photographs, both old and new, are one of the easiest and most effective ways to personalize a place. If you've gone digital, you can manipulate images with size and special effects. But even with a disposable camera, many photo labs can turn a favorite shot into an Ansel Adams sepia, a Warhol-like collage or a wall-filling poster.

Photo stylist Anna Davis has a treasured snapshot of her seven-year-old daughter Meagan riding the crest of a wave on her belly board at Waikiki Beach. She enlarged the shot to poster size and made it into a kind of triptych by cutting it into three sections, framing each in 12" x 36" stock frames. She hung them, spaced a few inches apart, above her desk.

"The exhilaration on Meagan's face is priceless," said Anna. "It gives the room such joy."

Make It Easy Care

> "Furniture should feel as personal as clothes. Every piece should be expressive, have unique character, and look as if it has always belonged."
> —Ralph Lauren

Rooms full of fussy furnishings and high-maintenance materials are fine if we have the time, desire and/or help to clean and care for them. But a poorly tended home not only looks sad and neglected, its occupants lose heart as well.

A home is part of the circle of life. We nurture it, fill it with comforts and love it into existence. As long as we keep it easy care, it will nurture and comfort us and be a place to love and be loved.

Break Free of Conventions

I had an interior designer colleague who had a charming little lake cottage done up in Pierre Deux fabrics, Ralph Lauren paints and refined vintage furnishings. One incongruous element stood out, however—a big glass coffee table top held up by a stuffed alligator. "I

> "I like houses to be cozy, comfortable and personal. Not cluttered, but filled with interesting objects and toys and as many jokes as I can get away with."
> —Candice Bergen

laughed out loud when I saw this in New Orleans," he said. "I figured I needed to laugh out loud more often, so I bought it."

Fashion designers Domenico Dolce and Stefano Gabbana surround themselves with furnishings in the trademark animal prints and saturated colors that dominate their women's wear lines. They've furnished their Sicilian vacation home as unconventionally as they do their runway collections with Moroccan paper lanterns, a carved wooden throne and local puppets that dangle from the ceiling beams. The crowning touch, however, is a pair of paintings above their bed portraying each as an early saint, halos and all. Said Gabbana, in an *InStyle* interview, "Each piece in the house is a piece of the story of us."

> "Tell me what you like and I'll tell you what you are."
>
> —John Ruskin, art critic

EXPRESS THERAPY

According to a *Cottage Living* study, 42 percent of the women the magazine surveyed said they express themselves through redecorating their homes. Thirty-four percent express themselves through making their own home improvements. Sixty-nine percent said they continually do little things to improve the look of their homes.

Trust Your Instincts

One of the perks of growing older is having the confidence to express who we are through what we choose to have around us. I've always liked white walls, for instance, because they look clean and are so benign. But I've never loved them. Gradually, those boring backdrops have morphed into the colors that my husband and I both relish, including russet, butter yellow and sage green.

The furnishings we've chosen to keep around all these years are a blend of Eastern and Western styles—sort of like our Amerasian family. And the only decorating rule we now follow is, whether it's a great big cabinet or a tiny teapot, we both have to love what we live with. The result is a comfortable place that reflects who we are and where we've been.

> "Personal style is best achieved by following your intuition and your heart."
>
> —Alexandra Stoddard

Live Life Now

> "Life is full of beautiful things. . . . It is up to us to make the most of them."
>
> —Howard Kushner, *When All You Wanted Isn't Enough*

We may long for candlelight and crystal dinners in the dining room, but when we're up to our elbows in diapers and Tippy-Cups, maybe that formal space would function better as a playroom, at least till the kids are past the food-flinging stage. Marissa Kim turned her dining room into a music room with a piano and cello for her children's daily practice.

"Since we only have big dinners on Thanksgiving and Christmas, we do a little furniture arranging in the living room and set up folding tables there," said Marissa. "Why let a perfectly good space go to waste 363 days a year?"

Satisfy Future Fantasies

Maybe we can't afford that midtown penthouse or that little place by the beach just yet, but we can plant the seeds of our dreams now.

Writer Celia Higgens longs for a garden of her own, but until she can afford a house with a yard, she satisfies her horticultural itch by puttering with the potted ferns and orchids that fill her small apartment.

Architect Carol Venolia tells of a friend who lived high up in a city apartment yet longed to live in the country. So she moved a couch to the balcony, created a privacy screen with potted trees and flowering shrubs, plugged in a small fountain to mask the street noise and, according to Venolia, spent many happy hours there.

Leave Your Imprint

Actress and singer Vanessa Williams incorporated her signature style into her home. She embedded bits of meaningful artifacts from her life in the fresh stucco of her powder room. The walls and ceiling are now a mosaic of her children's barrettes, the odd earring, shards from her first china pattern and her Miss America pin.

A reader of *Homestyle* wrote to the magazine about finding an old letter from the previous homeowners in the hollow base of a built-in pine kitchen table. It was addressed "To the family being raised here." The letter described the family, their history, ages and their life in the house. It signed off with the blessing, "We hope you find as much happiness in this house as we have." The new owners carefully replaced the letter and added one of their own addressed to a future family.

"In the end,
what affects your life
most deeply are things too
simple to talk about."

—Nell Blaine, artist

Before we wallpapered our powder room years ago, our then-teenaged nephew Maury and his friends made a time capsule out of it by noting their favorite rock bands and writing pithy statements all over the raw walls. Next time we paper any room, my husband and I will send our own message to the future.

Several Simple Ways to Personalize a Place

❀ Cluster a collection in one spot. Whether it's a flurry of snow globes on a mantle or a flock of rubber duckies on a bathroom ledge, it's the grouping of objects that gives them impact. Keeping that grouping in one place also keeps it from overrunning the house. My friend Ilene Spector has scores of silver-framed snapshots of her family. But instead of scattering them here and there, she's corralled them in a glass-enclosed étagère, so they're not only kept dust-free, they're given the prominence they deserve.

❀ Display a collection against a compatible background: crystal glistens in front of a mirror, leather-bound books look richer shelved on an old walnut bookcase and flowering houseplants look even brighter against a backdrop of botanical prints. I once propped a poster of Matisse's *Goldfish* behind a bowl of live goldfish. They looked quite content with each other.

❀ Consider snapping and displaying photos of meaningful places: a favorite beach, your grammar school, the bar where you met your beloved. I have a framed photo of my childhood church on a shelf in my bedroom. It's a rather ordinary looking structure, but it evokes vivid memories and reminds me of my roots.

❀ Add color and pattern to the kids' bedroom walls by framing book jackets from their favorite books in stock picture frames. Intersperse them with their own art that is simply glued on appropriately sized mat board. Use spray-on craft adhesive so your kids can easily peel off and update their artwork.

❀ Train mini muralists. Marissa Kim had her kids use their art skills and markers on the window shades in their rooms. Benjamin drew trucks and cars speeding along their edges, while his ten-year-old sister Molly crayoned hers with balloons, butterflies and horses. "The shades turned out so cute," said Marissa. "But they were so much fun to do, the kids can't wait until we buy new ones so they can try out other scenes."

❀ Paper a powder room or other small space with your homes' blueprints. We had a neighbor who wallpapered the walls of his tiny wet-bar with a set of his. The prints not only made a unique and highly personal backdrop, they could easily be referred to when locating an elusive water pipe or wall stud.

❀ Buy a lamp kit at a hardware store or home center, and turn a treasured teapot, pitcher or trophy into a reading light. When a heart warmer can be put to work, it doubles the pleasure.

❀ Encase a christening gown or other meaningful relic in a shadow box, and hang it somewhere significant. I once toured a designer showcase house that had recently been renovated

> "For where your
> treasure is, there will
> your heart be also."
>
> —Matthew 6:21

by a well-seasoned real estate tycoon and his much younger bride. Rooms were tastefully decorated in a spare, contemporary way. But the pièce de résistance was in the master bedroom, where the only art on the wall was in an acrylic shadow box above the big bed. There, like a prized trophy, was a lacy silk teddy—a tribute, apparently, to a monumental night.

DESIGN FOR LIVING

Mother Nature's Stencils

Use the leaves from a favorite tree for wall and furniture stencils. Art teacher Marissa Kim did just that when she plucked various-sized leaves from a sycamore outside her bedroom window. She flattened them overnight under a stack of heavy atlases, taped their backs (with nonmarring painter's tape) to the top and sides of an unfinished pine chest, then spray painted it a soft shade of green. She let the chest dry overnight, peeled off the real leaves and sealed the whole thing with a couple of coats of clear urethane.

The result? Wood-grained leaves in a wind-blown pattern that echoes Marissa's leafy view.

No yard? Adopt a pretty tree from a nearby park.

LIFE MATTERS:

The Heart at Home

Giving a home heart is a lot like giving ourselves to a relationship. It's a leap of faith, a trust in commitment, a belief in living happily ever after. Human relationships are fragile, but a home with heart will always love us back.